Perinatal Health Care
with Limited Resources

Staffan Bergström
Department of Obstetrics and Gynaecology,
Ulleval Hospital, Oslo, Norway

Bengt Höjer
Department of International Health Care Research (IHCAR)
Karolinska Institutet, Stockholm, Sweden

Jerker Liljestrand
Central Hospital, Karlskrona, Sweden

Ragnar Tunell
Department of Paediatrics,
Huddinge University Hospital, Sweden

MACMILLAN

First published 1994

Published by THE MACMILLAN PRESS LTD
London and Basingstoke
*Associated companies and representatives in Accra,
Auckland, Delhi, Dublin, Gaborone, Hamburg, Harare,
Hong Kong, Kuala Lumpur, Lagos, Manzini, Melbourne,
Mexico City, Nairobi, New York, Singapore, Tokyo.*

ISBN 0 – 333 – 59594 – 7

Printed in China

A catalogue record for this book is available from the
British Library.

Illustrations (unless stated otherwise) by Ulrika Westerstrand

Cover photograph courtesy of Ron Giling/Bazaar

Contents

Foreword   x
Preface   xii
Acknowledgements   xiv

1 Background and Epidemiology   1

The perinatal period   1
Registering pregnancies and outcomes of pregnancy   2
Perinatal care and population growth   3
The perinatal pathology of poverty   4
The road to perinatal health   5
FURTHER READING   6

2 The Normal Pregnancy   7

Psychological and social aspects of pregnancy   7
Health education   8
Antenatal care   10
   Risk identification and appropriate action/referral   12
   Prophylaxis and treatment   18
The antenatal card   19
Antenatal care components   22
FURTHER READING   22
REFERENCES   22

3 The Normal Birth   23

The place of birth   23
The birth assistant   25
Position during delivery and birth   25
Hygiene during delivery and puerperium   26
Basic delivery care   27
   Home deliveries   27
   Institutional deliveries   27
Supervision of labour   28
Monitoring the fetus   30
Avoiding man-made complications   30

FURTHER READING 31
REFERENCES 31

4 The Normal Newborn 32

Care of the baby 32
  Drying the infant 32
  Clean the airways 32
  Give the baby to the mother! 32
  Clamping and cutting the cord 34
The second clinical assessment 35
  Assessment of maturation and birth weight 36
  Circulatory and respiratory disorders 36
  Neurological disorders 36
  Infections 37
  Malformations 37
Prophylactic procedures 37
  Vitamin K 37
  Silver nitrate 38
  BCG vaccination 38
Avoiding man-made complications 38
FURTHER READING 39
REFERENCES 39

5 The Normal Puerperium 40

Maternal outcome 40
The first puerperal assessment 40
  Excessive vaginal bleeding 40
  Internal (abdominal) bleeding 40
  Signs of infection 41
  High blood pressure 41
The second puerperal assessment 41
  Vaginal bleeding 41
  Temperature 41
  High blood pressure 42
  Anaemia 42
  Breast-feeding 42
  Initiation of breast-feeding 42
  Breast-feeding problems 44
Maternal health education 44
Involving the father 44
FURTHER READING 45
REFERENCES 45

6 The Complicated Pregnancy 46

Anaemia 46

Importance and definition	46
Causes	47
Effects	47
Prevention	48
Management	48
Malnutrition	48
Diagnosis of general malnutrition	48
Effects	49
Management	49
Hypertensive disorders	50
Pre-pregnancy hypertensive disease	50
Non-proteinuric pregnancy-induced hypertension	50
Pre-eclampsia (toxemia)	50
Management	50
Pre-term labour	51
Epidemiology	51
Causes	52
Management	52
Prelabour rupture of the membranes pre-term	53
Management	53
Intrauterine growth retardation	53
Management	53
Breech presentation	54
Management	54
Twins	54
Management	55
Maternal haemorrhage	56
Placenta previa	56
Placental abruption	56
Diseases of the uterine cervix	57
Abdominal pregnancy	57
Management	57
Intrauterine fetal death	58
Causes	58
Management	58
FURTHER READING	58
REFERENCES	58
7 The Complicated Birth	**59**
Protracted delivery (dystocia)	59
Mechanical dystocia	59
Dynamic dystocia	61
Abnormal fetal presentations	62
Breech delivery	62
Tranverse lie at delivery	63

Twin birth   64
   Management   64
Placenta previa   65
   Management   65
Abruptio placentae   66
   Management   66
Bleeding from a non-contracted uterus   67
   Management   67
Bleeding from traumatic lacerations   68
Hypertension   69
   Management   69
Unconsciousness/convulsions   70
   Eclampsia   70
   Cerebral malaria   71
   Meningitis   72
   Cerebrovascular complications   72
Prolapse conditions   73
   Umbilical cord prolapse   73
   Prolapse of the cervix or inverted uterus 74
Retention of the placenta   75
   Management   75
Mental disease   76
FURTHER READING   77
REFERENCES   77

8 Immediate Neonatal Complications (Asphyxia)   78

Asphyxia at birth   78
   Strategies in the control of birth asphyxia 78
   Causes of asphyxia in the newborn 79
   Clinical signs of asphyxia in new-born baby 79
   Cleaning the airways   80
   Resuscitation scheme   83
   Assisted ventilation   83
   External cardiac massage   86
   Drugs   86
   Duration of resuscitation   86
   Post-asphyctic treatment   87
   Training for resuscitation procedures 87
Transport of pre-term or sick babies   87
FURTHER READING   88
REFERENCES   89

9 The Complicated Puerperium   90

Excessive bleeding and anaemia   90
   Management   90

Infections 91
   Management 91
Diseases of the urinary tract 92
   Lower urinary tract 92
   Upper urinary tract 92
   Trauma 93
   Over-extended urinary bladder 93
Hypertension 93
   Management 93
Psychological aspects 94
FURTHER READING 94

10 **Subsequent Neonatal Complications** 95
Respiratory disorders 95
   Wet lung disease (transient tachypnoea or pulmonary adaption syndrome) 95
   Respiratory distress syndrome (RDS, hyaline membrane disease) 95
   Meconium aspiration 96
   Congenital pneumonia 96
   Management 96
Low birth-weight babies 97
   Intrauterine growth retardation 98
   Pre-term babies 100
Hypothermia and neonatal cold injury 101
   Main causes of hypothermia 103
   Clinical signs of mild and severe hypothermia 104
   Prevention of hypothermia 105
   Treatment in hospitals 106
Nourishing the sick baby 107
   Breast-feeding 107
   Some properties of human breast-milk 108
   Alternatives to mother's milk 109
   Alternative feeding methods 110
   Supplementation of breast-feeding in pre-term babies 111
   Parenteral nutrition 111
Jaundice in the neonatal period 112
   Clinical judgement 112
   Assessing the degree of jaundice 113
   Jaundice in infants with special problems 113
   Treatment 114
Neurological disorders 115
   Symptoms of neurological disorders 115
   Causes 117
   Treatment of convulsions 117
   Prognosis 118

Birth trauma   118
   Subaponeurotic haemorrhage   118
   Fractures of the bones or epiphyseolysis   118
   Subcutaneous fat necrosis   118
Congenital malformations   119
FURTHER READING   119
REFERENCES   119

11 Perinatal Infections   120

Predisposing factors   120
   The mother   120
   The infant   121
Modes of transmission   121
Unspecific maternal perinatal infections   122
   Amniotic fluid infection syndrome   122
   Ascending infections after membrane rupture   123
   Puerperal infection   124
Specific maternal and fetal/neonatal infections in the perinatal
period   124
   Tetanus   124
   Malaria   125
   Tuberculosis   127
   Syphilis   128
   Gonorrhoea   129
   AIDS in adults   129
   AIDS in new-born babies   130
   Control of the spread of HIV   131
   Hepatitis B   132
   Other specific infections   132
Clinical picture of infections in the newborn   132
   Skin infections   132
   Conjunctivitis   133
   Bacteraemia in the newborn   133
   Meningitis   134
   Pyelonephritis   135
   Osteomyelitis   136
   Pneumonia   136
   Gastroenteritis   137
Prevention of perinatal infections   137
   Pregnant women   137
   The new-born baby   138
Management and antibiotic treatment   139
FURTHER READING   141
REFERENCES   141

12 Organisation of Perinatal Care 142

The setting and its actors 143
    Traditional birth attendants 144
    Midwives and nurses 145
    Medical assistants 145
    Doctors 146
    Community support 146
Different levels of perinatal care 146
    Antenatal care 146
    Pre-delivery care of high-risk women 147
    Delivery care 147
Neonatal care 151
Puerperal care 152
How to do it 152
FURTHER READING 155
REFERENCES 155

APPENDICES

  I Perinatal Terminology and Definitions 156

 II Vacuum Extraction 159

III Symphysiotomy 164

IV Caesarean Section under Local Anaesthesia 172

 V Blood-exchange Transfusion 177

VI Post-partum Family Planning 179

Index 183

Foreword

The past decade has witnessed a great deal of rationalisation of medical practice. Routines and procedures based on empiricism, and passed on from one generation to another are giving way to scientific scrutiny based on randomised clinical trials. Outmoded routines like nursery care for the newborn, delay in starting feeds for the newborn to allow for 'rest', pre-lacteal bottle feeds, and so on have given way to rooming-in, immediate feeding on the breast, and avoidance of feeding by the bottle. In the less developed countries, where access to scientific literature is often limited, progress is slow. Professor Bergström and co-authors of *Perinatal Health Care with Limited Resources* have identified the major scientific developments in perinatology, and have described how these principles can be applied using low-cost technology.

The authors have broken new ground in a number of ways. Many of the new routines and techniques have been associated with new technology. Labour wards and neonatal intensive care units in the more developed countries are nowadays crammed full with electronic gadgetry. The result has been that the cost of living for those born too soon or too small has escalated. It runs at between £5,000 and £10,000, depending on gestational age and presence or otherwise of complications. The less developed countries cannot afford such costs. The low-cost methods described in this book will enable the less developed countries to achieve marked improvements in perinatal care without incurring heavy costs.

It has been the general experience that the most cost-effective treatments are not necessarily those delivered by specialised hospitals, but by clinics, health centres and district hospitals. The health-care model of the more developed countries is based on the large urban hospital. New scientific developments in perinatology as they came to be applied in such institutions employed complex electronic technology. Less developed countries do not have to follow blindly and employ expensive gadgetry when scientific perinatal care can be provided using simpler and affordable technology. Sequential fundal height measurement as opposed to ultrasound, and 'kangaroo care' as opposed to incubators are two examples, among many.

If standards of perinatal care are to improve in the less developed countries the need is for a network of small scale health facilities to increase accessibility, and for well trained personnel to staff them. In most countries today, hospitals mop up between 40 and 80 per cent of public spending on health. In some countries a teaching hospital can consume more than one-fifth of the health budget. Even some resource-rich countries are facing stark economic necessity and closing down prestigious institutions to cut costs. Under the circumstances this book is all the more welcome because the common-sense approach described by the authors is applicable in the simplest of health facilities.

The daily routines and procedures in obstetrics and paediatrics are so uniquely different as to make the two departments separate lands which sometimes agree but most of the time have border skirmishes. Bearing in mind that the fetus has to travel only a short physical distance from the womb to become a newborn, there is a need for convergence of obstetrical and neonatal care. Such a convergence of views is another unique feature of the book. It is the outcome of a joint effort between an obstetrician and a paediatrician as well as other related disciplines. The convergence of approach has been well achieved, and the text moves smoothly from one discipline to another. This special quality of the book helps to put developing world perinatology in its right context.

The 1990s will be remembered as the decade of Safe Motherhood. A maternal death is a tragedy not only for the mother and often the newborn, but also for the surviving children. Between the Safe Motherhood Initiative and the Child Survival Revolution there remained the gap of Perinatal Care which this book so ably fills. In years to come it will continue to provide new standards against which countries can measure progress in perinatal care.

G.J. Ebrahim
Emeritus Professor,
Tropical Child Health,
University of London

Preface

During the last decades the cost of perinatal care and the development of complex, expensive technologies has demanded not only financial resources but also a technically advanced society for support and supplies. The economic situation both in developing and industrialised countries has made this explosion of cost and technology simply impossible.

For the vast majority of the world's mothers and new-born babies even basic perinatal care without technically advanced equipment is seldom available. When resources are limited it is wise and cost-effective to focus not on expensive equipment – like ventilators, sophisticated incubators or electronic monitors – but on making basic perinatal care optimal. This basic care is in our opinion not different in different societies. Good 'appropriate care' is good in Africa, Asia and developed countries such as Sweden.

Appropriate is a very demanding word, however. Something that may function in one setting may still be very inappropriate when seen in other settings. One example of this is the use of bottle-feeding with cows' milk formula. In developed countries bottle-feeding almost eradicated breast-feeding during the 1970s and in some countries almost every child grew up without being breast-fed. Such a routine may function fairly well under hygienic circumstances, where clean water and good bottles are available. When the same procedure was introduced in the third world it resulted in disaster. Unhygienic conditions resulted in diarrhoea, dehydration and infant deaths, and in 1981 WHO adopted a code of practice for marketing of breast-milk substitutes and promotion of breast-feeding. This has had the effect not only in the developing world but also in developed countries of re-establishing breast-feeding as the routine procedure for nourishing new-born babies.

There are many parallels to bottle-feeding, most of them introduced by Western medicine, very often contradicting the traditional perinatal care used for thousands of years.

One example is the habit of separating mother and child (normal, sick, pre-term, low birth-weight etc.) with the consequence that the mother does not get to know the child and cannot provide breast-milk. Mothers and children should be kept together. Another example is the use of incubators to keep babies warm. In developing countries they are ineffective and unhygienic and separate the child from the mother.

Some procedures, such as Caesarean section, are safe in developed countries, but not available in countries with scarce resources for the majority of parturients with obstructed labour. For more than a hundred years, symphysiotomy has been used as an alternative to Caesarean section in less severe obstructed labour cases but is generally not included in current teaching and not accepted to the extent it deserves. In this book the procedure is given attention, since we believe that an increased use of symphysiotomy would improve the condition for both mother and child, particularly in rural areas, and save many lives.

In the text we have tried to identify 'bottle-feeding-like' problems and suggested that such procedures should not be used when resources are scarce, despite the fact that they may function in developed countries under quite different circumstances.

Our intention with this book is, while respecting the scarce resources that limit clinical management, to add some information of practical value for doctors, nurses and midwives working with perinatal problems. We also hope to find readers among teachers in obstetric and paediatric care and their students. It is written in a spirit of stimulating active collaboration between all health workers in the perinatal period, such as obstetricians, paediatricians, midwives, nurses and traditional birth attendants. It is also written in the spirit of supporting active delegation of responsibility of perinatal care among these categories.

The authors are Swedish associate professors in obstetrics (S.B. and J.L.) and paediatrics (B.H. and R.T.) respectively. We have experience of working in clinical practice and research as teachers and consultants in several countries in Africa, East Asia and Latin America.

We assume that the reader has knowledge of basic facts in obstetrics and neonatology. The text does not go into details of anatomy and physiology relevant to the field of perinatal medicine. Rather, the focus is on appropriate technology and particular emphasis has been given to medicine not requiring sophisticated equipment.

The overriding objective of this book is to serve the needs of the mother and her newborn. The ethical implications can be said to correspond to the belief that our principal task is to **treat every pregnant women as if she were your own wife and the newborn as if it were your own child.**

Staffan Bergström
Bengt Höjer
Jerker Liljestrand
Ragnar Tunell

Acknowledgements

The authors gratefully appreciate support from the Swedish International Development Authority (SIDA), which facilitated the preparation and publication of the manuscript. Critical manuscript revisions have been most helpful and we particularly want to thank Professor George Povey, Maputo; Professor Kelsey Harrison, Nigeria; Associate Professor, Jan Wager, Saõ Tomé and Principe; Dr Jill Everett, London; Dr Susan Murray and Dr Carmela Green-Abate.

The authors also wish to thank Miss Liselotte Ehn, Mrs Eva Åsing-Johanson and Mrs Karin Törnblom for valuable and efficient secretarial help. Pharmacia Ltd most generously contributed by offering resources for drawing the figures. We thank Miss Ulrika Westerstrand for providing us with her artistic talent and patience, The International Child Health Unit (ICH) and the Department of Obstetrics and Gynaecology at the Academic Hospital, Uppsala, Sweden for their contributions towards the costs of production of the manuscript.

Staffan Bergström
Bengt Höjer
Jerker Liljestrand
Ragnar Tunell

1

Background and Epidemiology

The perinatal period

Let us consider two common perinatal scenarios:

A mother was to have her third child. When the labour pains started the father and the mother travelled to the health station. On the way to the health station the birth took place out in the fields. The mother and the child reached the health station and everything was all right, so the family was sent back home. The child started to suck and was quite well until the fifth day after birth. Then he developed a fever, refused to suck and had convulsions. He came to the only perinatal care unit in the country but after three days of treatment the child died with aspiration pneumonia and severe painful convulsions. This boy was one of 800,000 newborn babies who die each year due to neonatal tetanus. His mother is also one of the many women in the third world who has not received tetanus toxoid during her pregnancy.

During a home delivery of the fifth child a mother suffered severe pains, there was no progress in her labour and no delivery took place for 2 days. Suddenly her pains disappeared, the mother became pale and sick and after 2 days she was admitted to hospital. This mother died from septicaemia and shock and it was found that her uterus had ruptured 2 days previously. This mother was one of about 500,000 mothers who suffer a maternal death each year, mainly due to insufficiencies that could have been overcome even with prevailing limited material resources.

These two scenarios demonstrate perinatal disasters occurring several thousand times a day. In most countries in the third world 60-100 infants per 1000 live births die during the first year. Of these, about half are deaths that occur during the first week after birth – neonatal mortality. In most countries there is an equal number of stillbirths. This means that about 8-10 million babies die each year before birth (stillbirths) or soon after birth (neonatal deaths).

1

In most developed countries the infant mortality is 6-10 per 1000 live births. During the neonatal period 4-5 die per 1000 and an equal number are stillborn.

There is thus a tenfold difference between developed and developing countries today. Neonatal asphyxia, tetanus and other infections as well as increased mortality due to low birth-weight are the predominant causes of neonatal deaths. An increased awareness of risk factors during pregnancy, good training in resuscitation of asphyctic babies and prophylactic measures to avoid infections are the main factors that could improve the high risk of death among mothers and children in the perinatal period.

A motherless child will have little chance of survival. It is remarkable that the risk of maternal death was less in Sweden a hundred years ago than it is in most developing countries in the world today. This reflects the low status of women and girls in most countries today – resulting from discrimination against girls from an early age and, consequently, a lack of food, lack of education, excessive work, and also inadequacy of prevention and treatment of acute potentially fatal occurrences such as bleeding, infections and eclamptic convulsions during pregnancy and delivery. There is a slow growing awareness of these disasters; and a reduction in maternal deaths is one of the goals accepted by UNICEF in 1991[1].

In most textbooks the 'perinatal period' corresponds to the time surrounding birth. More exactly the World Health Organization (WHO) has recommended the following definition: '**The perinatal period** is the one extending from the gestational age at which the average fetus attains the weight of 1000 g (equivalent to 28 completed weeks of gestation) to the end of the seventh completed day of life.' No reference is made to anything other than antenatal/postnatal age. More specifically it should be noted that 'perinatal' alludes neither to the fetus/neonate nor to the pregnant/puerperal woman. Thus, even if 'perinatal period' is global in the sense of covering events during a well-defined period of time, current use of 'perinatal' in practice excludes most maternal aspects by focusing on fetal/infant events. Maternal morbidity or mortality in the perinatal period is normally not included in the scope of 'perinatal medicine'. In this book, however, the focus will be on both the principal actors in the perinatal period, the pregnant/puerperal woman and her fetus/newborn.

Registering pregnancies and outcomes of pregnancy

Thorough description of the course of perinatal events does not necessitate computers but an efficient and complete **manual collection** of perinatal data. In order to facilitate comparisons between different parts of a country, different countries and differences over time periods a terminology that is generally accepted must be adhered to. In Appendix I we give the perinatal terminology recommended by WHO in some detail.

It is a recognised fact that the stillbirth rate and the neonatal mortality rate are difficult to measure. In many countries, particularly in rural areas, a baby who dies is a 'non-event' and is buried without being registered either as a birth or as a death. The **complete registration of every perinatal death** in an area is important in order to develop appropriate perinatal programmes.

Improving conditions for survival of mother and newborn implies not only collection of data but subsequent analysis and interpretation. The local data must be presented so that health workers collecting them have adequate feedback. A revision of events, in cases of maternal or neonatal death or complications, is called **perinatal audit**. It means that mismanagement and inadequate routines are discussed and methods to counteract and correct them are established so that improved clinical norms can be achieved.

Perinatal care and population growth

In many parts of the world lack of food is one of the most important health problems. Between 30 and 40 per cent of pre-school children may have moderate, and one child out of 20 may have severe signs of malnutrition in some impoverished countries. The supply of food simply does not satisfy the basic needs of the population today. Unfair distribution aggravates impoverishment and maintains malnutrition. In most poverty-stricken societies children are economic assets and represent the sole source of security for the parents. In some studies from African countries 85 per cent of women interviewed state that their latest pregnancy was a desired one. There seem to be no shortcuts in the strategy to reduce the rapid global population growth. The desperation in the confrontation with this reality has even led some Western experts to advocate that no further steps be taken to reduce infant deaths.

What impact would improved perinatal care have on the number of children surviving? Would such perinatal care have an adverse (growth-accelerating) impact on the population? There is no evidence that improved perinatal care increases population growth. The reason is probably that breast-feeding is enhanced and prolonged if the child survives and a prolonged contraceptive effect is achieved. The spacing of births is improved. The tendency to replace dead children is decreased when the number of dead children is reduced. However, broad programmes aiming at reproductive health, and family planning, must be carried out. Emphasis should be given to health education starting in schools well before children reach puberty, and to antenatal and postnatal clinics, where both health supervision and family planning services can be offered.

Experience shows that a safe motherhood and a safe perinatal period with surviving infants and **prolonged breast-feeding** are cornerstones upon which vigorous family planning activities should be initiated. By **intensified female education** and improved reproductive health there is some hope that confidence in the small family norm will be gained among the poor of today.

The perinatal pathology of poverty

Even if the absolute number of individual deaths among pregnant women is much lower than among fetuses/newborns we should bear in mind the key position of the mother in the family. In one study from Bangladesh more than 95 per cent of all infants born to mothers who died were themselves dead before attaining 5 years of age. This fact together with the well-known fact that 99 per cent of all maternal deaths in the world occur in poor countries constitute the hallmarks of the perinatal pathology of poverty.

In the field of maternal mortality there is almost always one of four principal etiologies behind a death: **eclampsia, haemorrhage, obstructed labour** or **septicaemia. Eclampsia** is the result of poor surveillance of pregnancy-associated hypertension, which may lead to proteinuric hypertension (pre-eclampsia) and if not treated and managed correctly, to eclampsia. **Haemorrhage** is principally a puerperal complication, though placental problems (placenta previa or placental abruption) before delivery may contribute to haemorrhagic death. **Obstructed labour** complicated by a ruptured uterus usually belongs to this group, though it causes a minority of haemorrhagic deaths. **Septicaemia** is mainly a post-partum problem due to a genital infection acquired either during pregnancy (ascending intrauterine infection) or transmitted by health staff at delivery. It may also be transmitted by unhygienic manipulation related to clandestine abortion which is a prominent cause of maternal death in many areas.

The perinatal pathology is almost always associated with maternal disease. One important common denominator in this pathology is low birth weight (LBW). This is particularly important in most of the Asian countries where 20-30 per cent of newborns have a birth-weight below 2.5 kg. The etiological pattern prevailing in poor countries is different from that prevailing in affluent countries. In third world countries the bulk of the LBW problem is associated with a combination of factors including maternal malnutrition, anaemia, malaria, placental insufficiency, pre-eclampsia and other unknown factors.

Perinatal infant deaths have a wide variety of causes. Maternal malnutrition and vulnerability to infections, particularly genital infections, seem to play a predominant role in most poor countries. Such maternal infections may lead to uterine contractions and finally to expulsion of the baby, either pre-term or at term, sometimes with intrauterine growth retardation (IUGR). Asphyxia and infections, especially neonatal tetanus and hypothermia are other causes of neonatal death.

The perinatal pathology of poverty has its roots in poor reproductive health of the mother. Women of reproductive age are exploited sexually, physically and economically, and the multiple deprivation of fundamental prerequisites for health and well-being constitutes the roots of the problem of poverty-related diseases and deaths in the perinatal period. The severe economic downturn in the early 1980s affected perinatal health in a negative way in many parts of the world (Figure 1).

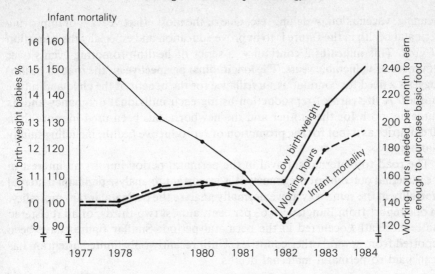

Figure 1   'The perinatal pathology of poverty' can be illustrated in many
ways. Infant mortality and prevalence of low birth-weight are
two indicators influenced by this pathology. The severe
economic downturn in the early 1980s affected vulnerable
groups in the third world most markedly. In this example from
Brazil poverty is expressed as monthly working hours needed
for purchase of basic food. (From: Becker, R. and Lechtig, A.
Increasing poverty and infant mortality in the northeast of
Brazil. *Journal of Tropical Paediatrics* 1987; **33**: 58-9.)

The road to perinatal health

The road to health in the perinatal period requires above all a healthy mother.
Her health during pregnancy depends on a number of circumstances related
to her living conditions before becoming pregnant and particularly before
puberty. The young girl living under adverse conditions during childhood will
be more likely to develop malnutrition (skeletal stunting), deficiency diseases
(rickets) and/or infections (e.g. polio resulting in a limp and pelvic asymmetry).
Such a young girl will often run a high risk of becoming pregnant in her teens
and – if attaining the perinatal period – entering the perinatal period as an
obstetrically high-risk case. The road to perinatal health is threatened by a
number of complications potentially affecting either the mother or the fetus
or both. Either of the two may die from complications with origins and roots
in the woman's early years. The road to death is paved with a large number
of stones laid up to decades before a life comes to an end in the perinatal period
– the mother's or the child's.

'The road to future perinatal health' starts with the newborn and in particular
the newborn girl. It denotes an active interest in following and guaranteeing
the maintenance of health by a number of prophylactic measures, breast-feeding,

weaning, vaccination, weighing, etc. One of the most effective ways of improving perinatal health in the future is to improve education and especially the education of girls. This indicates a continuity, a series of health-promoting events over a number of vulnerable years. The **longitudinal perspective** in 'the road to health' suggests a need for continuous surveillance for the benefit of the child and future mother. A **life card** of reproduction listing each individual pregnancy and its outcome, both for the mother and the newborn, has been used in more than 30 countries as a tool for the promotion of reproductive health, including family planning.

The road to maternal survival in the perinatal period implies an interest in the maternal outcome of pregnancy. It is important to analyse **perinatal maternal mortality** in the same way as we normally analyse the perinatal infant mortality. In one report from Bangladesh 63 per cent, almost two-thirds, of all registered maternal deaths occurred in the perinatal period. Similar figures have been reported from several other countries. Until recently only limited attention has been paid to perinatal maternal deaths.

FURTHER READING

1.   UNICEF *The State of the World's Children 1991*. Oxford University Press: Oxford, 1991.

2

The Normal Pregnancy

Psychological and social aspects of pregnancy

A woman's first childbirth represents her passage from one phase of life (daughter, unmarried, childless) to another (mother, wife). This change in her identity has psychological and social as well as biological aspects. She will rely primarily on her own personal network – family, friends, religious support, traditional practitioners – during this passage. This personal network will have more local and cultural variation than is found in medical care. It is important to recognize that a woman's personal network and background is the framework within which medical care must adapt.

The relative importance people give pregnancy and childbirth is reflected by a variety of local traditional practices and beliefs, many of which are important for the 'social bonding' of a new-born child. Medical perinatal care must respect and if possible take advantage of these traditional practices and beliefs. Massage of the pregnant woman, dietary restrictions during pregnancy and various modifications of the desired behaviour of the pregnant woman are examples of such traditional beliefs and practices, as well as many of the practices of traditional birth attendants. These traditions focus on the woman and her pregnancy, and initiate extra attention for the family to be. Such traditional practices must be respected, provided they are not clearly harmful or dangerous. The wide variety of harmful practices that does exist is not usually best counteracted by condemnation, but rather by a continuous dialogue between traditional practitioners and a modern health-care system.

The health of mother and newborn is to a great extent determined by non-medical factors in society. The strongest of these determinants is **women's access to education**. The reasons for this appear to be that women who have gone to school have greater ability, and a higher capacity to influence their own lives.

The **status of women** in a society is also a significant determinant of perinatal health. Women's groups and organisations play an important role in improving the status of women, thereby increasing focus on female health and perinatal health. The role of men and fathers is also important, as well as the presence of, or possibility to develop, informal or formal parental education. The opinions of family decision makers, e.g. grandmothers or maternal uncles, may be crucial in many issues related to perinatal health.

Putting **women's health in focus** is thus an extremely important goal when trying to improve perinatal health. As practically all societies have traditional ways of caring for the pregnant woman, it is often advantageous to relate to such traditions when focusing on women's health. Health education and antenatal care are two important perinatal fields where this is evident.

Health education

Young people expecting a baby are particularly open to health information. The arrival of a new family member makes us contemplate our own life-style. Of course we are particularly eager to learn how to preserve the health of the baby (Figure 2). It is therefore useful to combine all contacts between the health-care system and the parents, and even the extended family, with health information. Antenatal care services, maternity homes, parental classes, maternity wards, well baby clinics and vaccination campaigns are all examples of occasions that

Figure 2   Pregnancy and childbirth are very important events to everybody. This can be used in perinatal care.

must be used to spread knowledge of health matters. Person-to-person contact individually or in small groups, is often the best way to communicate. 'To communicate' should be a dialogue and not a speech by one person to another, and it is wise to start from the experience and problems of the individual pregnant woman, see Figure 3.

Figure 3   Organising perinatal care should include instructional training to staff on how to behave in front of perinatal women. Such training should focus on empathy and respect. Blaming a woman with reproach and guilt does not help that woman to feel confident. Perinatal care means showing interest in listening and understanding, which are key elements in empathy.

There are many subjects that are important to discuss in order to improve perinatal health: what to eat during pregnancy, why work should be reduced in the last trimester, why the mother should attend the antenatal clinic, how and why to take iron/folic acid and malaria tablets, and where and how to give birth are all important aspects of antenatal health education.

Breast-feeding practices, child immunisations, child nutrition, family planning, hygiene and other aspects of preserving child health are of interest to most parents.

Questions of life-style are becoming increasingly important in perinatal health education: smoking, drinking and sexual habits. Sexually transmitted diseases, including syphilis and AIDS, pose a rapidly increasing threat to newborns and their mothers, thereby threatening perinatal health and indeed the reproductive capacity of a society. This fact, and how to avoid sexually transmitted disease, is a very important topic of health education for men, women, adolescents and decision makers worldwide today.

Antenatal care

Even provision of very simple, cheap and basic antenatal medical care has a dramatic impact on maternal and neonatal health, measured either as mortality or morbidity. The provider of care – nurse or midwife – is the first link in medical care in the perinatal period and as such is an extremely important person. The attitudes, experience and knowledge of the antenatal care provider will determine the health of many mothers and children.

An essential point in antenatal care is **early booking**. An early first visit during pregnancy gives the nurse or midwife a chance to get to know the pregnant woman, inspire confidence, transmit knowledge, detect risk and take appropriate action. Even with extremely simple and cheap antenatal care, early booking is a crucial factor.

Another essential point is the risk approach. 'Something for everyone but more for those in need' is a WHO expression illustrating the risk approach. 'Something for everyone' should here mean a minimum of 1-2 antenatal care visits for every pregnant woman. Figure 4 gives an example of content of antenatal care if a woman has only one visit. In these few visits a careful but rapid risk assessment must be included. High-risk women – 'those in need' – must be recommended to have additional antenatal care visits, specific prophylaxis/treatment, special delivery care, or a combination of these.

While the actual **causes** of raised obstetric risk consist of an often complex combination of socio-economic, biological, environmental and health-care determined factors, certain simple but useful **indicators** of heightened risk are described below.

A pregnant woman with an indicator of heightened obstetric risk is more likely to develop complications during pregnancy/birth/puerperium than a woman with no such risk ('low-risk woman'). This is, of course, a matter of probability:

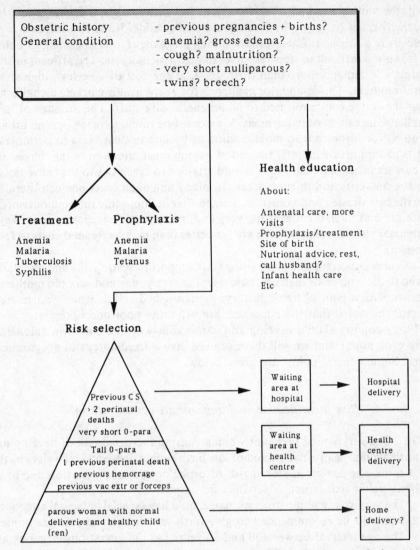

Obstetric history   - previous pregnancies + births?
General condition   - anemia? gross edema?
                     - cough? malnutrition?
                     - very short nulliparous?
                     - twins? breech?

Treatment   **Prophylaxis**

Anemia   Anemia
Malaria   Malaria
Tuberculosis   Tetanus
Syphilis

Health education

About:

Antenatal care, more
visits
Prophylaxis/treatment
Site of birth
Nutrional advice, rest,
call husband?
Infant health care
Etc

Risk selection

Previous C S
> 2 perinatal
deaths
very short 0-para

Tall 0-para
1 previous perinatal death
previous hemorrage
previous vac extr or forceps

parous woman with normal
deliveries and healthy child
(ren)

Waiting
area at
hospital

Waiting
area at
health
centre

Hospital
delivery

Health
centre
delivery

Home
delivery?

Figure 4   If a woman presents herself for antenatal care only once during
her pregnancy, the above figure summarises the important actions
to be taken. Note that neither weighing, symphysis – fundus
measurements, fetal heart auscultation nor blood pressure measurements are included in this basic antenatal visit.

a woman with strong indicators of increased obstetric risk ('high-risk woman')
may still have an uneventful, unassisted childbirth at home, while the low-risk
woman may develop an unexpected, potentially fatal complication. In spite of
this, it is evident that high-risk women should receive extra perinatal attention
and care, to optimise the use of limited health care resources.

Increased risk may be defined further: is it an increased risk for the baby (e.g. the mother has had several previous low birth-weight deliveries), for the mother herself or for both? One should also consider if the risk increase is at delivery (e.g. previous Caesarean) or during pregnancy (grave anaemia), or both.

It is often difficult to steer resources to high-risk mothers. The affluent urban group will demand more than their share, at the cost of voiceless, high risk, rural mothers. This is a major challenge for every health worker, a challenge that should be communicated to all antenatal care staff. The message of this challenge is: **care in outlying areas**. Ways must be found to reach beyond urban centres, for instance with mobile units, or by intermittent visits to peripheral units to support their staff. Instead of paying most attention to the 'haves' in urban areas any antenatal care should attempt to reach out to the 'have-nots' on the outskirts and in rural areas. In many antenatal units one can literally see the best dressed and nourished women first in line, while the malnourished, illiterate and ill-clad come at the very end, perhaps only at closing time. **Few antenatal visits to many women are far better than many antenatal visits to few women.**

It is also important that supervising staff support the extra visits and attention given to the women of high obstetric risk: the very young and very old mothers, women with a poor obstetric history, malnourished and anaemic women etc. It must be noted that these mothers are often the poor and illiterate.

Every country should develop and continuously evaluate its own antenatal care programme and we will therefore not give a fixed antenatal programme here. Some general points are given below.

Risk identification and appropriate action/referral.

AGE   The very young pregnant woman runs an increased risk of developing anaemia during pregnancy, and of low birth-weight delivery. If she gives birth at term, she has an increased risk of cephalopelvic disproportion due to a bony pelvis that is not as yet fully developed.

The very young nulliparous woman should have special antenatal attention and should be recommended to give birth at a health unit, not at home.

The age interval between 20 and 30 years has the lowest obstetric risk as far as age is concerned. Above this age interval there is a gradual increase in risk, a risk often combined with a risk of high parity.

OBSTETRIC HISTORY   The number and outcome of previous pregnancies are of utmost importance. The nulliparous woman has evidently not yet been tested in her birthing capacity, and has a higher risk than a woman having her second or third baby with previous normal deliveries. After the low risk second and third childbirths there is a gradual risk increase with rising parity, however. After 5-6 births the risk has reached the same level as that of the nulliparous woman, and with higher parities the risk gradually increases even higher. The risks with high parities include more atypical fetal positioning at birth, uterine inertia (= more difficult labour, and more postpartum bleeding), more hypertension and renal problems, and sometimes greater anaemia. Short birth intervals more severely increase the obstetric risk, especially due to increased frequency of iron-deficiency anaemia.

The common attitude of 'just one more routine birth' must be counteracted and 'the overconfidence in multiparity' altered to a vigilant attitude at delivery of grand (6+) multiparous women.

One often overlooked fact is that **multiparity is a threat to maternal health only in impoverished societies with high child mortality rates**[1]. In affluent societies grand multiparous women run a very small or insignificant risk of maternal death. It is not **multiparity** that kills but **poverty**.

A description of previous births gives useful information on the risks for the pregnant woman at the coming birth. In general, any serious previous delivery complication in a particular woman indicates that she should give birth under medical supervision rather than at home. Of particular importance is a previous operative delivery. A previous Caesarean section signifies a particularly high risk at any later childbirth, and motivates delivery in a hospital with operative facilities.

HEIGHT   There is an association between maternal height and delivery outcome, at least in part due to increased risk due to a small pelvis in a very short woman (Figure 5). Nulliparous women below 146 cm of height in Tanzania have been shown to have an increased risk of disproportion at delivery and are therefore considered high-risk mothers for whom hospital delivery is recommended[2]. The cut-off point for such recommendations must be analysed locally.

CONSTITUTION   A limp, resulting, for example, from childhood polio or trauma, as well as spinal deformity, indicate increased risk at the first childbirth.

TISSUE PALLOR   Maternal anaemia is a common complication of pregnancy. Even limited haemorrhage at birth may be fatal in the gravely anaemic woman. An important routine of any antenatal care service is therefore to detect anaemic women by careful inspection of the inside of the lower eye-lid, or of the tongue or palms of hands (Figure 6). One study showed that the majority of cases with anaemia with a packed cell volume (PCV) <25 per cent were diagnosed through clinical examination while almost no women with normal PCV were classified as being anaemic[3].

OEDEMA   Foot and leg oedema is so common at the end of pregnancy that it has practically no value as a risk indicator. Generalised oedema, gross oedema or rapidly developing oedema, particularly in the face, are warning signals of pre-eclampsia, however, and should lead to careful blood pressure recording and urine analysis for proteinuria.

BLOOD PRESSURE   A raised blood pressure during pregnancy means an

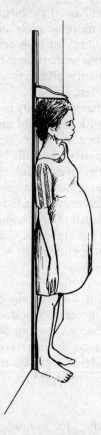

Figure 5   A short nulliparous woman has an increased obstetric risk.

Figure 6   An interested observer will by rapid but careful examination of the
conjunctivae detect the vast majority of grave anaemias (haemoglobin
<90 g/litre). If the examined woman has irritated conjunctivae
(conjunctivitis, smoke in the eyes from cooking), check tongue or
palms instead. Serious anaemia leads to engorged veins, leg
oedema and strained breathing.

increased risk for mother and child, especially if the hypertension is a component of pre-eclampsia (see page 50).

A high blood pressure is not, however, easy to detect, interpret, or manage. **First**, because a well-functioning blood pressure apparatus is often not available in the antenatal unit, nor experienced staff to use it. **Second**, because a blood pressure recording from early pregnancy is usually not available for comparison. **Third**, because the normal blood pressure range varies between different populations. **Fourth**, because pre-eclampsia often develops very rapidly: the chances of detecting pre-eclampsia by measuring blood pressure during a few, far-between antenatal care visits are small even if all women are examined at every visit. This will be particularly true if pre-eclampsia is rare, as in some areas.

So, when should one spend valuable staff time measuring blood pressures, should apparatus be available?

1. It is wise to get one blood pressure recording from every woman as early in pregnancy as possible. Hypertensive women can then be given extra attention; and pressure recordings will be available for all women for comparison in late pregnancy.

2. Check blood pressures of all nulliparous women at every visit in the last trimester, as they run a higher risk of pre-eclampsia than parous women.

3. Measure blood pressure in the last trimester when one of the following pre-eclampsia-suspect symptoms appear: rapid oedema development, generalised or gross oedema, headache or blurred vision.

4. Measure blood pressures of certain high-risk women: with a history of previous pre-eclampsia/eclampsia, or with previous perinatal deaths of unknown origin.

Standardising blood pressure measurement routines in an area, training and retraining staff in these routines, and maintaining clear management schemes in cases of pregnancy hypertension are important tasks for the persons in charge of antenatal care.

PROTEINURIA   Antenatal visits in the Western world, at least in the third trimester, have until now included as routine urine analysis for proteinuria for early detection of pre-eclampsia. This is presently being questioned. In pre-eclampsia, proteinuria very rarely starts before the development of hypertension, and urine analysis may thus be unnecessary as long as the blood pressure is normal. In the developing world, many women have chronic proteinuria due to previous schistosomiasis (bilharzia), and this makes urine analysis difficult to use in the detection of pre-eclampsia. Repeated urine analysis is worth while in the last trimester in women with an increased risk of pre-eclampsia: women with hypertension, renal disease or generalised oedema.

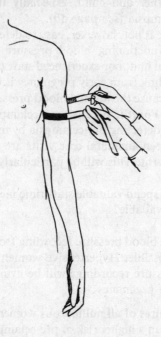

Figure 7   The mid-upper-arm circumference is a practical screening method
for malnutrition during pregnancy. The problems of incorrect
scales and relationship to the duration of pregnancy, as well as the
bias of leg oedema, are avoided by using this method.

MALNUTRITION   Indicators of malnutrition are clinical condition, low pre-
pregnancy weight, small weight increase, inadequate weight:height ratio and
small **mid-upper-arm circumference**. While judgement of clinical condition
may be useful with some experience, all methods using weighing have
drawbacks – incorrect scales, time needed, necessity of relation to height etc.
To measure the circumference of the relaxed and hanging upper arm is a rapid
way of assessing nutritional status in crowded antenatal care services (Figure
7). At national level, such measurement of a few hundred non-pregnant
women, when related to weight:height tables, provides an adequate basis to
allow minimum mid-upper-arm circumference to be used by district nurses
or midwives as an indicator.

For instance, in Mozambique a mid-upper-arm circumference in a pregnant
woman below 23 cm is a very reliable indicator of malnutrition and a
circumference of 23-25 cm means a moderate risk of malnutrition[4].

COUGH   A cough of more than a few weeks duration should lead one to
suspect pulmonary tuberculosis. Prompt diagnosis and treatment will
dramatically reduce the risk of infecting the baby at birth, as described in
Chapter 11 page 127.

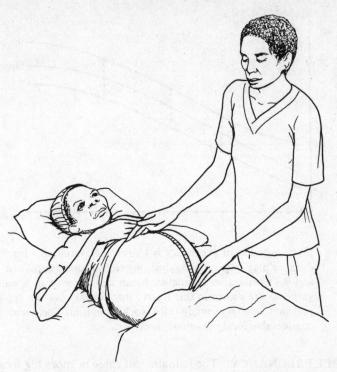

Figure 8 Symphysis – fundus measurements must be performed according to a correct method: the woman flat on her back with extended legs, the examiner measuring from the top of the symphysis pubis to the highest point of the uterus on its long axis.

FETAL GROWTH   In the last trimester of pregnancy, measurement of the **symphysis – fundus distance** gives a reasonable impression of fetal size (Figure 8). When plotted on a graph it will be a valuable instrument in well-trained hands for monitoring fetal growth (Figure 9). Twins or hydramnion may be the cause of a high symphysis – fundus measurement, while intrauterine growth retardation may be suspected with subnormal recordings. A fairly exact knowledge of the gestational age is essential for the use of symphysis – fundus curves, however. Furthermore, several observations at different occasions are often necessary for interpretation. In a crowded antenatal unit, fetal growth monitoring is therefore best reserved for high-risk women.

ATYPICAL PRESENTATIONS   The manual detection of breech presentations and other atypical fetal positions (transverse or oblique) requires considerable experience. Detection is very important, however, as breech presentations at birth carry, for instance, a very high perinatal mortality in inexperienced hands. Therefore, timely referral to hospital delivery is important if external version is not carried out (see page 55).

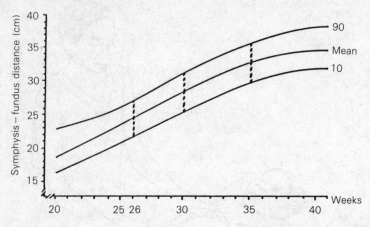

Figure 9 If the duration of pregnancy is known the symphysis – fundus
distance may be plotted against duration of pregnancy, and 10th
and 90th percentiles calculated. Mean and range of such a normal
variation are shown in this figure, that roughly may be applied to
pregnant women in many third world countries. There may be
considerable local variations, however.

MULTIPLE PREGNANCY   The palpation of three or more big fetal parts or
a high symphysis – fundus distance should lead one to suspect a multiple
pregnancy. Women with twin pregnancies should receive extra antenatal
attention – iron, folic acid, antimalarials, rest and reduced work load – and
delivery should take place where qualified help is present. Multiple pregnancy
always signifies an increased perinatal risk.

SOCIAL RISK   It must be recognised that poor, illiterate, single mothers run
a higher risk of perinatal complications than affluent, educated women with
stable marriages. Whether such social risk indicators are registered on the
antenatal card or not, all staff of antenatal care units and delivery units must
be aware of the need to give underprivileged mothers extra time and support.

Prophylaxis and treatment

IRON, HOOKWORM TREATMENT, FOLIC ACID   The prevention or treatment of maternal anaemia is a common component of antenatal care all over
the world. With the exception of a few well defined areas, iron intake during
pregnancy is too low to maintain the pre-pregnancy iron balance. A newly
delivered woman has reduced iron stores and often clear signs of anaemia
if she has not taken iron tablets during pregnancy. Where hookworm is an
important contributing cause to pregnancy anaemia, antenatal routine should
include hookworm treatment for all women or for all anaemic women.

While the need for iron supplementation during pregnancy is almost global, the need for extra folic acid is local and depends on dietary habits, cooking habits and malaria. See paragraph on anaemia in Chapter 6 (page 46).

TETANUS TOXOID   It is sad that hundreds of thousands of babies die every year of tetanus, when the infection can be easily and cheaply prevented by vaccinating the mother twice during pregnancy.

Injections should be given with an interval of 1-2 months, the last one at least 4 weeks before the estimated time of delivery. Just one dose of tetanus vaccine does not give good protection against tetanus, and it is therefore important that all mothers are given **two injections**.

MALARIA SUPPRESSION   As is described on page 126, malaria resistance is reduced during pregnancy. In malaria-endemic areas, prophylaxis or suppression of malaria is an important component of antenatal care. The rapidly changing malaria situation in the world makes permanent recommendations impossible. Drugs used are discussed on page 126.

SYPHILIS SCREENING   In areas where syphilis is common, a serum analysis for syphilis screening is probably the most important serum analysis one can perform during pregnancy. The antenatal care unit must be able to follow up positive tests with treatment of the woman and her husband, see page 128.

HIV   Some antenatal care services include serological HIV (human immunodeficiency virus) screening, at least of high-risk groups. To be meaningful such testing must be combined with some kind of action (counselling, abortion possibility).

The antenatal card

The paper on which data are registered for a pregnant woman should be designed in a way that helps the nurse/midwife to decide when to take a specific action and also what action to take. For instance, on the antenatal card from Tanzania (Figures 10 and 11) it can clearly be seen what to do when a woman is found to have a raised blood pressure or other abnormal finding. This is called **an action-oriented antenatal card.**

Asking the pregnant woman to look after her antenatal card carefully between antenatal care visits is often the best way of having access to the information at the next visit, at delivery or when a complication occurs.

An antenatal card covering all the pregnancies of a woman has been introduced with success in many countries. This card is kept by the woman over the years, and has space for the various antenatal visits and births. It gives rapid information on the woman's history when she visits her antenatal unit or comes for delivery, and thereby facilitates individualised treatment. It has proved[5] to be an invaluable instrument in improving perinatal health, and deserves to be adopted everywhere.

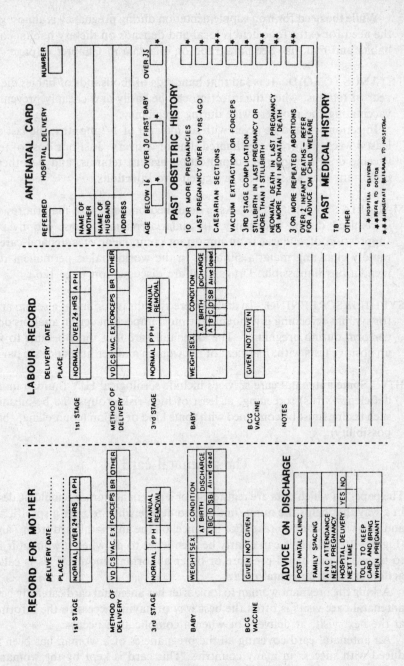

Figures 10 and 11 Both sides of the action-oriented antenatal card of
Tanzania. At the bottom one can read that one star
indicates hospital delivery, two stars referral to doctor,
and three stars immediate referral to doctor.

FIRST VISIT ONLY

HEIGHT BELOW 146 cms [ ] * LIMP OR POLIO LEG [ ] *

HISTORY OF COUGH FOR OVER 4 WEEKS SEND SPUTUM FOR TB TEST [ ]

ADVICE ABOUT WEANING [ ] ADVICE ABOUT DIET [ ]

HISTORY	DATE OF VISIT						
	BLEEDING SINCE L.M.P ***						
	OTHER SYMPTOMS						
EXAMINATION	VERY ANAEMIC ***						
	BP IF OVER 140/90 ***						
	OEDEMA AND PROTEIN ***						
	FUNDAL HEIGHT						
	FOETAL HEART						
	FOETAL LIE Br * Tr * Vx						
	VERY BIG OR SUSPECT TWINS *						
TREATMENT	IRON						
	FOLIC ACID						
	CHLOROQUINE						
	TETANUS TOXOID						
	OTHER DRUGS						
ADVICE	ABOUT PLACE OF DELIVERY						
	ABOUT HOW TO TAKE TREATMENT						
	DATE OF NEXT VISIT						
	TOLD TO BRING CARD						
TESTS	Hb						
	PROTEIN IN URINE						
	SPUTUM FOR TB IF POSITIVE ***						

NAME _____

PATIENT SUMMARY

	NORMAL	WRITE DOWN RISKS
PAST HISTORY		
THIS PREGNANCY		

* HOSPITAL DELIVERY
** REFER TO DOCTOR
*** IMMEDIATE REFERRAL TO HOSPITAL

OTHER COMMENTS

_____
_____
_____
_____
_____
_____
_____
_____
_____

Antenatal care components

While the importance of antenatal care for perinatal health is unquestionable, the contents of the care provided can be discussed. Which components are most important? What is the optimal number and time interval of routine antenatal visits? What indicators of high risk should be used, and what action should they lead to? How should quality of care be evaluated? These issues are increasingly being discussed in developed countries. It appears important to analyse which parts of antenatal care should be developed and which may even be left out, thus leaving fixed 'inherited' programmes. This is an important field of international research.

The way to study the various risk factors and interventions of antenatal care scientifically is to study two groups of pregnant women. One group has had the treatment or risk factor and the other has not. Is there a statistical difference? The study can be performed by following two groups of pregnant women, a so-called **prospective study**. It is much easier to perform a retrospective **case – control** study, however. A group of women with a certain complication is selected, for instance, in a busy delivery unit, and compared with random controls (that is, women without the complication). The two groups are then compared for the particular treatment or risk factor. In this way every item of an antenatal care programme should ideally be studied.

FURTHER READING

1. Rooney, C. *Antenatal Care and Maternal Health: How Effective is it? A Review of the Evidence*. WHO: Geneva, 1992.

2. De Maeyer, E.M. *et al. Preventing and Controlling Iron Deficiency Anaemia through Primary Health Care*. WHO: Geneva, 1989.

REFERENCES

1. Harrison, K.A., Rossiter, C.E., Tan, H. Family planning and maternal mortality in the Third World. *The Lancet* 1986; **i**: 1441.

2. Everett, V.J. The relationship between maternal height and cephalopelvic disproportion in Dar es Salaam. *East African Medical Journal* 1975; **52**: 251-6.

3. Liljestrand, J., Bergström. S. The value of conjunctival pallor in the diagnosis of pregnancy anemia in Mozambique. *Journal of Obstetrics and Gynaecology of Eastern and Central Africa* 1992; **10**: 45-6.

4. Liljestrand, J., Bergström, S. Antenatal nutrition assessment: the value of upper arm circumference. *Gynecologic and Obstetric Investigation* 1991; **32**: 81-3.

5. Shah, P.M., Shah K.P., Belsey, M.A. *et al.* The home-based maternal record. *IPPF Medical Bulletin* 1988; **22**: 2-3.

3

The Normal Birth

The place of birth

In the third world the majority of deliveries take place at home with a traditional birth attendant assisting the mother. In such cases the traditional birth attendant may even spend several days with the family, also helping after the actual delivery with the woman's personal hygiene and housework. It is not surprising that even mothers recognised as 'high risk' may prefer to give birth at home together with their families. Other reasons for preferring a home birth are cultural traditions concerning delivery and handling of the placenta and of the child. Fear of surgical procedures such as episiotomy or Caesarean section is perhaps another factor counteracting institutionalised delivery care.

A wise approach to this conflict is not to counteract the work of the traditional birth attendant, but to improve and develop institutionalised delivery care so that traditional values are respected as far as possible, and so that unnecessary interventions are avoided. Possible ways of improving co-operation with traditional birth attendants are discussed in Chapter 12.

On the other hand, statistical data from several third world countries as well as historical data from industrialised countries show that reducing perinatal mortality is very difficult without increasing the number of deliveries taking place in institutions.

Institutional delivery services all over the world face a great challenge in trying to respect a woman's social and psychological background. Paradoxically, one often sees today more such respect in a small peripheral unit, for instance in a health centre or small hospital, than in a big, urban, highly specialised obstetric unit.

An important study performed in Guatemala city is an example of this: In a big labour unit half the nulliparous women were assigned a 'doula' to accompany them during delivery[1] (Figure 12). The other half of the nulliparous women had no such company and were mainly alone during

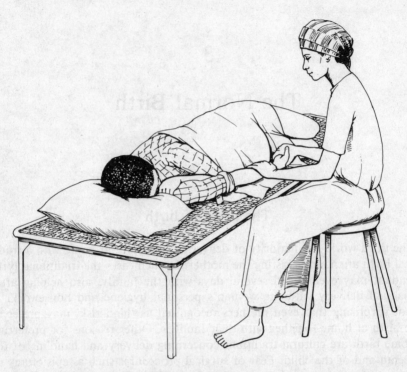

Figure 12   The presence of an accompanying person during labour gives
              significantly shorter labour, less oxytocin use, and fewer obstetric
              interventions.

dilatation. The doulas had no medical education and had the sole task of
providing company and comfort to the woman in labour. The study showed
significantly shorter labour, less use of oxytocin and fewer obstetric interventions among the women accompanied by a doula than among the women
left alone.

Empathy is thus a keyword. **Empathy means emotionally putting yourself
in the other person's position, trying to feel what the other person feels in a
difficult situation.** Overcrowding together with lack of staff and equipment
may cause strained conditions and incorrect routines. Supervisory staff
must emphasise empathy even under such conditions, and help in devising ways
of promoting such care. Are traditional birth attendants used fully? Can
women in labour have an accompanying person (mother, sister etc)? Are all
routines necessary, and respectful to women? Is mother – child bonding being
promoted? How are contacts with the patient and her family handled if
complications occur?

The birth assistant

Few women give birth without any help at all. The birth assistant is the primary health worker in perinatal health care. 'Primary' here meaning most important.

The largest number of perinatal complications will be found among low-risk pregnancies and low-risk births because such births are so numerous. High-risk births have, of course, high complication rates, but being much fewer in number cause fewer deaths or handicap than low-risk births. **Most maternal deaths occur in low-risk groups.** Many delivery complications are quite unpredictable, for instance, cord prolapse, haemorrhage or puerperal septicaemia. The birth assistants with medical training (nurse, midwife, health assistant etc.) and without medical training (traditional birth attendant) are therefore the people to be supported, inspired, educated and retrained in any real effort to improve perinatal health.

Position during delivery and birth

Investigations in recent years using modern equipment have clearly shown the negative effects of placing women in bed during delivery and birth. When the mother lies down during the dilatation phase, the delivery will be slower and the risk of fetal asphyxia will be higher than if she walks around. When she lies flat on her back the uterus compresses the great blood vessels in the abdomen, thus contributing to a decreased oxygen transport to the fetus. When lying down she also loses the gravitational effect of the baby pressing downwards, which speeds up delivery when the mother walks around.

When the time comes for bearing down and expelling the baby, a woman lying flat on her back in the so-called gynaecological or lithotomy position will literally be forcing the baby up-hill, working against gravitation. The expulsion phase will be longer and the risk of asphyxia higher during expulsion, than if she chooses some other position.

Delivery will be safer and faster if the woman giving birth can walk around or sit during dilatation. The safest and fastest expulsion normally occurs if the woman can choose the birthing position she prefers when bearing down. Standing, sitting, half-sitting or on all fours are positions well-known from traditional birthing care, and these positions are today successfully being used in modern obstetric care (Figure 13).

It is worrying to learn that traditional birth attendants in some countries, have started to use the gynaecological position at childbirth, once introduced by Western medicine, because 'that is how they give birth in hospitals'. The change should be in the opposite direction. Traditional birthing positions are today being rediscovered in the Western world, as they have also proved to be better in certain cases of difficult delivery such as breech presentation.

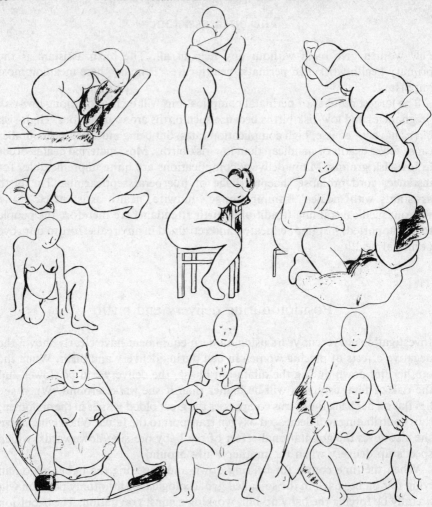

Figure 13   The delivering woman should be encouraged to attempt the least
uncomfortable birthing position. (Illustration courtesy of Midwife
Inga-Lena Olsson)

Hygiene during delivery and puerperium

During home deliveries hygiene is one of the most important factors for perinatal
health. Washing hands before assisting the delivery is very important, and should
be performed with soap and water. If clean water is not at hand, water should
be boiled before washing. Cleaning the nails of the birth attendant with a nail-
brush or clean stick is desirable. The woman giving birth must not give birth
on a dirty floor or on the ground. A clean mat or clean newspaper should be
used on the floor to protect the woman and her baby from infection. If the
birth attendant performs vaginal examinations, hygiene of the hands is even
more important and must be very carefully performed (Figure 14).

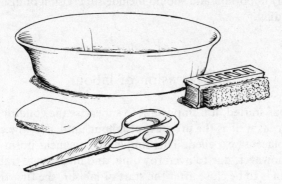

Figure 14　Careful hygiene of the birth assistant's hands is an essential, but often forgotten, part of birthing care at home deliveries as well as in institutionalised deliveries.

In institutional delivery care hygiene is also essential. Overcrowding plus lack of soap and water may otherwise largely counteract the benefits of institutional delivery care. Routines for cleaning, disinfection or sterilisation of equipment and buildings must be upheld, as well as hygiene routines during delivery and puerperium. Special aspects of hygiene include the care of the newborn, the umbilicus, and maternal lesions as well as protection of staff against such infections as HIV.

Basic delivery care

Home deliveries

Improvement of the safety of home deliveries can only be achieved through collaboration and dialogue with the birth assistants, be they either traditional birth attendants or field health workers. Education and supply of basic equipment – soap, nail-brush, oil cloth, razor blade or scissors, string, gauze, disinfectant – are important components of such collaboration.

Institutional deliveries

An important component when trying to improve perinatal health is critical analysis of the basic, or normal, institutionalised delivery care. Are basic, simple routines adequate? Are the admission routines correct? Can staff correctly distinguish between **false labour** (latent phase) and **active labour** (dilatation phase)? Is active labour adequately monitored? The role of the physician or head midwife in supervising the routines of normal delivery care and puerperal care is extremely important and should include supervision of dismissal routines and breast-feeding.

Supervision of labour

When labour has started, it is important to supervise **the condition of the fetus and the mother,** as well as **the progress of labour** until after the child has been born and the placenta expelled. This simple management norm is not always easy to fulfil, however, due to overcrowding, and inadequate training of staff.

If supervision is to be close after the start of labour, the first thing to define is: when can one safely say that labour started? Labour has started when the following three criteria have been met:

Frequency of contractions: 3-5 per 10 minutes.
Duration of contractions: 30-90 seconds.
Intensity of contractions: moderate or strong.

When all three criteria have been met, labour is regarded as adequate; when only one or two have been met, labour is regarded as inadequate.

With the start of adequate labour, the use of a graphic illustration of the progress of labour has proved to be a fundamental aid in the safe and early recognition of dystocia (prolonged delivery).

It is important that a graphic illustration is as simple as possible in order to facilitate its utilisation in practical delivery care. The **cervicogram**[2] is a simplified partogram and an alarm system in order to make early recognition of dystocia possible and practical (Figure 15). The dilatation of the cervix is a measure of risk, dictating the action to be taken.

When dilatation has reached 4 cm (start of the **active phase**), the cervicogram can be used. Any dilatation of the cervix of less than 4 cm can be regarded as representing the **latent phase***.

When a delivering woman has reached 4 cm (or more) the palpated cervical diameter is indicated at the time 'zero' (Figure 15). On the same line (the current dilatation) the **'alert line'** is drawn 2 hours to the right of the time of the first palpation with a slope corresponding to a dilatation of 1 cm/hour. The **'action line'** is then drawn 2 hours to the right of the alert line and with the same slope. The time difference between the two lines is thus 2 hours.

After the two lines have been drawn on the cervicogram the woman is examined every 2-4 hours depending on circumstances. The vast majority of delivering

---

*The conventional limit, at which dilatation the active phase of labour is said to start, is 3 cm. However, the most crucial decision is to settle whether or not active labour has **actually** started. Therefore, Bird and other authors defend 4 cm as more practical than 3 cm. We recommend this routine: there will be few parturients with a dilatation of 4 cm not in active labour, but a significant number of (parous) parturients with a dilatation of 3 cm, not yet in active labour.

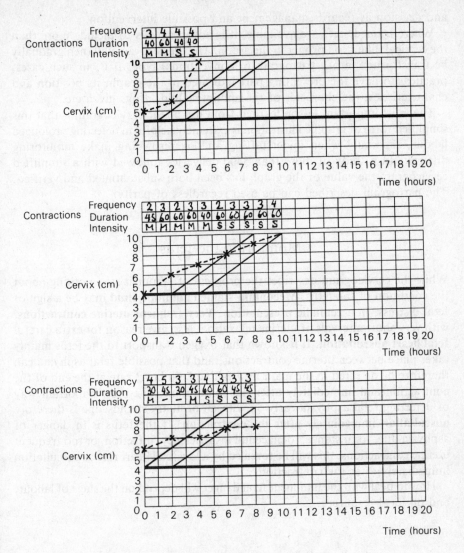

Figure 15 Three examples of partograms/cervicograms.
Frequency is number of contractions per 10 min. Duration is in seconds. M = medium, S = strong.
Top: Normal cervicogram. Cervical dilatation slightly faster than 1 cm/h. *Middle:* Suspicious cervicogram. Cervical dilatation line crossing 'alert line'. *Bottom:* Pathological cervicogram. 'Alert line' and 'action line' crossed.

women will have the progress of the cervical dilatation to the left of the alert line and empirically 98 per cent will be positioned to the left of the action line. When the alert line is crossed it is wise to prepare transport to hospital. The 2 per cent of women who also cross the action line require a careful assessment, and decision as regards management and possible intervention.

Where trained staff are available, it is advantageous to include more than the cervical dilatation proper in the graph. The cervicogram will then gradually be transformed into a partogram of conventional type. It is, in such cases, practical to have the presenting part indicated in the graph, its position and characteristics, the character of the amniotic fluid, drugs given etc.

The most important lesson learned from use of the cervicogram is that this simplified form of graphic illustration is extremely helpful in detecting prolonged labour, especially when understaffing and overcrowding make monitoring difficult. In a study of more than 5400 deliveries followed with a simplified cervicogram the value of the graph has been both substantiated and verified. The partogram described can be used regardless of parity.

Monitoring the fetus

While the cervicogram describes the progress of labour it says nothing about the condition of the fetus. **Meconium-stained amniotic fluid** may be a sign of fetal distress, in a cephalic presentation. **Very frequent uterine contractions**, with very short intervals of uterine relaxation, also give reason for extra careful **fetal heart auscultation**. It is known that oxygen transport to the fetus mainly takes place between uterine contractions, and that possible fetal asphyxia can therefore be detected in the main by a falling fetal heart rate at the end of the contraction and immediately after the contraction. The most important way of detecting fetal asphyxia early on with an ordinary stethoscope is therefore **auscultation immediately after the contraction**. If the fetus is in danger of asphyxia due, for instance, to placental insufficiency, infection, or too frequent uterine contractions, this will be revealed by a low fetal heart rate at auscultation immediately after the contraction.

How to deal with the imminent fetal danger will depend on the stage of labour, and on local resources.

Avoiding man-made complications

We have a special responsibility **not only to assist normal labour and birth, but also to teach how to avoid the abnormal**. A number of complications are frequently the result of obstetric malpractice in many labour units in the world. Examples of such malpractice are:

● forced cervical dilatation in spite of normal labour progress;

● artificial rupture of the membranes without a valid indication;

● external pressure on the woman's abdomen or uterine fundus in cases of uterine inertia before the cervix is fully dilated;

● routine use of episiotomies, for instance, in all nulliparae;

● forcing the woman to bear down even though the head is high, and the woman has no urge to bear down;

● physical violence to 'non-cooperative mothers';

● forcing the expulsion of the placenta by pressure and traction before placental detachment.

FURTHER READING

1. The Partograph, I The principle and strategy II, A user's manual, III Facilitator's guide. WHO: Geneva, 1989.

REFERENCES

1. Klaus, M.H., Kenell, J.H., Robertson, S.S., Sosa, R. Effects of social support during parturition on maternal and infant morbidity. *British Medical Journal* 1986; **293**: 585-7.
2. Bird, G.C. Cervicographic management of labour in primigravidae and multigravidae with vertex presentation. *Tropical Doctor* 1978; **8**: 78-84.

4

The Normal Newborn

Care of the baby

Drying the infant

The evaporative heat loss from the skin results in a lowering of skin temperature by 3-4°C within seconds after birth. This is the most intense of the sensory stimuli provoking spontaneous breathing at birth. The heat loss is both necessary and impossible to avoid. But if cooling by evaporation continues in the minutes or hours that follow, the body temperature will drop below 35°C and hypothermia will occur. Thus drying of the baby is necessary and it is also important to change the first wet towel to a dry one.[1]

Clean the airways

In a normal delivery with clean amniotic fluid there is no need to clean the mouth and throat by suction or wiping. The normal child swallows the contents of the mouth before the first breath. A simple and safe method for assisting the child is to place its head down in the prone position (See Figure 16).

Give the baby to the mother!

Every birth attendant should be aware of the fact that a new-born baby is a person with neurosensory behaviour; the capability to see, hear, feel (pain, warmth, cold), smell, taste and cry out (happily or unhappily). Bearing this in mind, we should treat every new-born baby as a human being.

Several studies have shown that for the mother the first few hours after birth are a special and sensitive period, and that this period is important for the

32

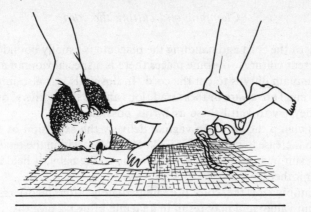

Figure 16   Cleaning the airway by placing the baby in the prone position and head down.

promotion of maternal bonding[2]. Separation of the child from the mother for a day or two disturbs this sensitive period and may have a detrimental effect on the mother's care of the baby and, more importantly, breast-feeding. Sadly, such separation is routine in many hospitals.

When the baby has been dried, he should be wrapped in a cloth to avoid heat loss and given to the mother. She may put him to the breast, which will give her the opportunity to watch the baby and to touch him. Within 15 minutes most babies will start to try to find the nipple of the mother's breast in order to try to suckle. Such early breast-feeding results in:

1. Release of oxytocin in the mother which promotes uterine contractions and helps to prevent post-partum haemorrhage.

2. Improved performance with stimulated milk production in breast-feeding.

3. The mother being able to observe the baby continuously. Is he/she active? Does he/she suck? Is he/she limp or blue?

The high neonatal morbidity and mortality in developing countries is largely the result of the combined effect of hypothermia, infections acquired at delivery or contact with staff or other children and of non-functioning breast-feeding. This is prevented by giving the child to the mother and letting the two stay together. Thus, in many countries the support of **early contact between mother and child** is one of the most urgently needed changes in hospital care routines in the perinatal period. The baby could e.g. be carried by the mother in direct contact with her skin, under her clothes, during the day. This is called the **kangaroo method.**

Only in cases where the immediate neonatal assessment results in the decision that the baby needs resuscitation or other medical treatment, or where the mother is unable or unwilling to see her own baby, is separation of mother and child at birth justified.

Clamping and cutting the cord

The cutting of the cord and handling the placenta is usually bound by tradition in the different cultures. In some places there is a special woman attending the birth whose main duty is to cut the cord. In hospitals it is also important that health personnel are aware of these traditions and of the mothers' own requests, and that they try to fulfil these as far as possible.

When to clamp the cord? In vaginal delivery the expulsion of the placenta results in an increase in pressure, up to 40-50 mmHg, within the fetal circulation. This may result in a fast placental transfusion to the baby, if held in a position below the mother.

Early clamping of the cord (i.e. immediately after birth) results in low haemoglobin values and may result in anaemia after 1-2 months. On the other hand, too late clamping of the cord results in hypervolaemia and possibly hyperviscosity of the blood (packed red cell volume >70 per cent in central venous blood)[3], which may lead to respiratory difficulties and volume overload of the heart. If the newborn baby is placed on the mother's breast, the cord could be left un-clamped until the pulsations have disappeared, without an increase of the haemoglobin value of the infant.[4]

Thus, clamping of the cord at **approximately 1 minute after birth** seems to be most advantageous.

How to clamp and cut the cord? **Inelastic closing material** such as **ties, strings** or **bands** are commonly used. However, this old widely used procedure results in a very temporary closing of the vessels. As early as ½ to 1 hour after birth the shrinkage of the cord loosens the band and reopens the vessels, increasing the risk of both bleeding and infection.

The most accurate method of clamping the cord is to use a **rubber band**. After clamping the cord with a forceps and cutting it, the rubber band is applied around the cord with the help of a forceps (see Figure 17).

In many developed countries a plastic cord clamp is used. This is expensive, is not reusable, and thus inappropriate for use in developing countries. The advantage is that it effectively closes all vessels in the umbilical cord and can be removed within minutes or hours after birth.

CUTTING THE CORD   A clean instrument such as a razor blade, a scalpel or a pair of scissors should be used. The procedure should be carried out as a surgical procedure, using sterile instruments.

SUBSEQUENT HANDLING OF THE CORD   The normal cord must be kept clean and dry. The simplest and most widely used method of treating the cord is to leave it open and uncovered. There are several disadvantages with the use of cord bandages. They may easily be soiled by urine or meconium and tend to moisten the cord. Also, traditional measures such as applying cow dung, ashes etc. can lead to umbilical infections and death.

The daily use of antiseptics such as 'triple dye', hexachlorophane or chlorhexidine during the first week has been shown to control the colonisation

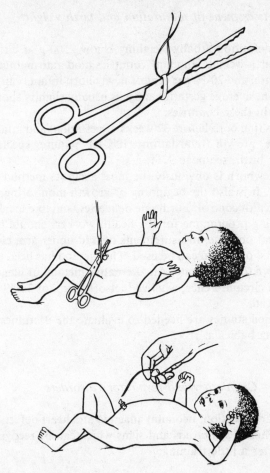

Figure 17 A simple, reliable and inexpensive method of tying the cord with a rubber band.

of bacteria, especially that of *Staphylococcus aureus*. On the other hand, there is no controlled study proving that any of these agents has any effect on the frequency of septic infection in the newborn. These procedures are widely used today, however, and there is a need to undertake studies in this field.

The second clinical assessment

A systematic assessment of the child should be performed before the baby is transferred to the maternity ward or before the midwife leaves after a home delivery. The aim of this examination is to find out if the child needs special neonatal care.

Assessment of maturation and birth weight

By international definition a baby weighing below 2500 g at birth is defined as having a 'low birth-weight'. In many countries moderate malnutrition of the fetus is very common and 20-30 per cent of newly born infants can be classified as 'low weight'. The average gestational age is usually slightly shorter than the normal 40 weeks in these countries.

Pre-term infants (i.e. born before 37 weeks of gestation) and infants suffering from intrauterine growth retardation (IUGR) require special attention immediately after birth, see page 97ff.

Weighing the newborn is obviously the most accurate method of assessing the baby's weight. It is also the beginning of growth monitoring and thus an essential part of health control. For home deliveries, suitable locally produced scales and a training programme for the health workers should be provided.

If weighing is not possible, measurements of **mid-upper-arm circumference** with 'cut-off points' of 8-9 cm can be used. The method has been used in some countries and shown to be accurate. An alternative method of identifying high-risk babies is chest circumference, where a 'cut-off point' of 28-29 cm has been found to be accurate.

Locally performed studies are needed to evaluate the usefulness of various methods of finding babies at risk.

Circulatory and respiratory disorders

Impaired pulmonary function, neonatal anaemia and heart defects resulting in cyanosis all give clinical symptoms and signs which can be recognised by any birth attendant after a little training:

1.   Is the colour normal or pale or cyanotic? (Also look inside the lip.)

2.   Is the respiratory frequency normal (fewer than 60 breaths per min)? Is it regular or irregular?

3.   Are there respiration retractions (see page 95) in the chest or not?

4.   Is there grunting (see page 95) respiration or not?

If any of these signs are present there is a need for close observation of the child and possibly transferral of the child to a hospital.

Neurological disorders

During the first 2-3 hours after birth a normal new-born baby will fall asleep and start crying in response to external stimuli only. The child will move its arms and legs in big smooth symmetrical movements. A child exposed to perinatal asphyxia will often have a period of neurological overstimulation during the first few hours after birth, with hyperactive shaky movements and intense crying. There is a risk that this condition will lead to convulsions and it should accordingly be regarded as an early sign of a possible neurological disorder.

Infections

Clinical signs that may indicate infection and which require additional checking are: lack of sucking efforts on the breast of the mother; changing general condition with fever or subnormal temperature; lack of spontaneous movements; failure to breath continuously with periods where breathing is absent and heart rate slow (apnoea).

Malformations

Severe malformations are often obvious and easily visible on external examination of the new-born baby. Some of these are not compatible with life. In some cases corrections are possible at high technology surgical centres. In field practice in most developing countries it is, however, not possible to save the life of infants with herniation of the spinal cord, severe umbilical hernia, severe brain malformations etc. The external inspection of the baby should be extended to include an examination of the palate. Cleft palate may give rise to feeding difficulties. It is thus wise to make sure that the palate is intact before the first meal is given.

Prophylactic procedures

Vitamin K

A neonatal deficiency of vitamin K exists in about 0.5 per cent of all new-born babies in industrialised countries, and especially in pre-term babies. In developing countries the frequency is higher and it is even more important to give prophylactic vitamin K. Oral administration of 2 mg vitamin K has been shown to be almost as effective as injection with 1 mg. From a hygienic and economic point of view, the use of oral vitamin K is therefore recommended. The risk of gastrointestinal or other types of neonatal bleeding is especially high in pre-term babies, and small for gestational age babies. All these babies should receive vitamin K prophylaxis.

Silver nitrate

There are good reasons for continuing to use 1 per cent silver nitrate as eye prophylaxis in regions with a high frequency of gonorrhoea. The alternatives, 1 per cent tetracycline or 0.5 per cent erythromycin ophthalmic ointments or drops, are also recommended. The efficacy of the different substances seems to be similar[5]. The main disadvantage of silver nitrate is that it leads to a chemical conjunctivitis which interferes with the visual responsiveness of the child. Routine prophylaxis with silver nitrate is therefore no longer practised in the Scandinavian countries or in the United Kingdom.

BCG vaccination

In every country where there is a significant risk of acquiring tuberculosis, BCG vaccination with 0.05 ml vaccine should be given intradermally (Figure 18). In the case of a hospital delivery, the vaccine should be given before discharge.

Avoiding man-made complications

In many hospitals **the baby** is nowadays routinely separated **from the mother** immediately after birth. This is inhumane and might even be dangerous since the mothers may become reluctant to come to hospitals to give birth.

The baby is very often left wet after delivery until the placenta is delivered. The midwife then cuts the cord, and puts the wet baby on the weighing scale, washes the baby and sends it to a nursery. If the baby is not dried and put in a warm place or with the mother, 80 per cent of infants will develop **hypothermia**

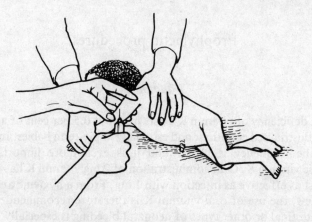

Figure 18   BCG vaccination against tuberculosis is given by an intradermal injection of the vaccine in the left arm/shoulder.

(i.e a rectal temperature below 36°C). Hypothermia and **neonatal cold** injury are one of the main reasons for neonatal deaths in developing countries (see page 101).

Another effect of this treatment is that, after a few hours, the infant will be exposed to the **bacterial flora from the hospital staff** instead of from the mother. This is risky since the mother produces antibodies to the bacteria of her gastrointestinal tract and breast-milk also contains such antibodies.

Some traditional measures increase the risk of colonisation of the babies' skin with bacteria from people other than the mother or from contaminations like soil. **Use of invasive procedures** such as umbilical catheterization may also be risky.

Feeding practices vary in different countries. **Feeding alien food-stuffs** such as butter may result in abdominal discomfort and colonisation by pathogenic bacilli. The widespread habit of throwing the colostrum away deprives the baby of useful nutrients.

FURTHER READING

1. Ebrahim, G. J. *Care of the Newborn in Developing Countries*. Macmillan and ELBS: London and Basingstoke, 1979.

2. Roberton, N.R.C. *A Manual for Normal Neonatal Care*. Edward Arnold: London, 1988.

REFERENCES

1. Dahm, L.S., James, L.S. Newborn temperature and calculated heat loss in the delivery room. *Pediatrics* 1972; **49**: 504-13.

2. Klaus, M.H., Jerauld, R., Kreuger, N. C. *et al*. Maternal attachment – importance of the first post-partum days. *New England Journal of Medicine*. 1972; **286**: 460-63.

3. Philis, A.G.S. Further observations on placental transfusion. *Obstetrics and Gynecology* 1973; **42**: 334-43.

4. Nelson, N.M., Enkin, M. W., Salgas S. *et al*. A randomized clinical trial of the Leboyer approach to childbirth. *New England Journal of Medicine* 1980; **302**: 865-70.

5. Hammerschlag, M.R., Cummings, C., Roblin, P.M. *et al*. Efficacy of neonatal ocular prophylaxis for the prevention of chlamydial and gonnococcal conjunctivitis. *New England Journal of Medicine* 1989; **320**: 760-72.

5

The Normal Puerperium

Maternal outcome

There are two stages in the assessment of the puerperal woman: the **first assessment** immediately after the expulsion of the placenta and the **second assessment** within 24 hours after birth.

The first puerperal assessment

The first assessment aims at observing the following aspects:

Excessive vaginal bleeding

Observe whether there is bleeding, even slow, from the vagina immediately post-partum. It is important to certify that the uterus is **contracted** by palpating the lower abdomen.

Internal (abdominal) bleeding

Even if there are no signs of external (vaginal) bleeding any tissue laceration in the birth canal (immediately outside the uterus and the vagina) may give rise to a dangerous leakage of blood. **Checking the pulse** will show if circulatory collapse is imminent (rapid and weak pulse). Such patients are also **pale** and it is important to check for **tissue pallor** (conjunctivae, tongue or palms).

Signs of infection

Careful **hygiene** must be observed both in health units and at home. Assessment must focus upon early signs of endometritis – myometritis such as moderate fever (below 38°C), slightly exaggerated uterine pain and foul-smelling vaginal discharge. A history of many hours of amniotic fluid leakage, a difficult delivery or unclean manipulation increases suspicion of infection.

High blood pressure

Even in cases of normal blood pressure during pregnancy, high blood pressure may occur after delivery. It is therefore wise to measure post-delivery blood pressure as routine. This is particularly important if there is any sign of blurring of the consciousness. About 25 per cent of eclampsia cases occur after delivery (almost always within 48 hours).

The second puerperal assessment

When the time has come for the midwife to leave the home or the mother to leave the health unit the second assessment should be carried out for early detection of the following complications.

Vaginal bleeding

As in the first assessment, any bleeding in excess of what is compatible with normal lochiae should be noted. Such bleeding may be a warning sign of impending **uterine infection** (endometritis – myometritis), which can worsen and result in genital sepsis, a dangerous complication that may lead to **maternal death.**

Temperature

Puerperal infection with fever is particularly **dangerous**, since it is most often associated with genital infection leading to septicaemia (bacteria in the blood). Any fever must be analysed carefully and treated accordingly. The possibility of puerperal malaria must also be borne in mind. It is important to note any foul smelling of the lochiae, which may indicate intrauterine infection. A **contracted uterus** is also important to note, since a non-contracted uterus is more prone to become infected. Any **uterine tenderness** is also most important as an early sign of infection of the uterus. A puerperal woman with **fever** should never be allowed to be left unattended before she has received adequate treatment. In any case such women must be examined **daily** till the fever has disappeared.

High blood pressure

Any blurring of consciousness or headache should lead to a blood pressure check before discharge because of the risk of hypertension.

Anaemia

Conjunctival pallor and pale tissues in general are signs of anaemia. Such women should be checked carefully for loss of blood or any other cause of anaemia in the puerperal period.

Breast-feeding

During the first week after delivery the mother may need assistance while establishing breast-feeding. A smooth and successful initiation of breast-feeding is one key component for the survival of a child in a developing country since:

> Breast feeding is a unique process that provides ideal nutrition for infants and contribute to their healthy growth and development; reduces incidence and severity of infectious diseases, thereby lowering infant morbidity and mortality; contributes to women's health by reducing the risk of breast and ovarian cancer, and by easing the spacing between pregnancies; provides social and economic benefits to the family and the nation; provides most women with a sense of satisfaction when successfully carried out.[1]

Initiation of breast-feeding

A healthy baby will, if given the opportunity, start sucking the breast within 15-30 minutes after delivery. This, and every consecutive time the child sucks the nipple, will stimulate the release of milk secretion hormone, prolactin. Oxytocin also makes the uterus contract after delivery, which diminishes the bleeding.

Although milk will not be produced by the breasts until 2-3 days after delivery it is important that the baby is given the opportunity to suck very soon after birth and then whenever he shows that he wants to suck the breast.

The sucking technique is important. The baby's body should be kept close to the mother and the mouth attached to the nipple – well open and sucking the whole areola of the breast (Figure 19). If the baby does not suck in a good position (Figure 20), the mother should take it from the breast and try again.

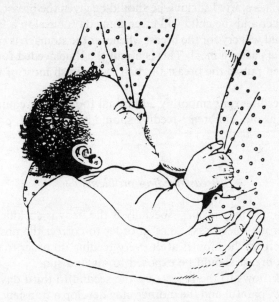

Figure 19 Baby sucking in good position. (From Savage King, F. *Helping Mothers to Breast Feed*. AMREF: Nairobi, 1992)

Figure 20 Baby sucking from the breast in a bad position as if he is sucking from a bottle. (From Savage King, F. *Helping Mothers to Breast Feed*. AMREF: Nairobi, 1992)

In many countries a new-born baby is given fluids such as sugar water, honey or butter as the very first feed. Such customs may introduce harmful bacilli to the intestines and cause abdominal discomfort. On the other hand colostrum (the very first, yellowish and thick milk produced by the mother) is often discarded. This is a pity since colostrum contains a lot of protein and other nutritious substances as well as antibodies. It has been shown that any additional fluids or other food given to the baby increases the risk of acquiring diarrhoeal diseases several times[2]. Promotion of exclusive breast-feeding is thus a high priority issue.

All attempts to promote undue use of milk formulas, e.g. by offering the mothers free samples, is a crime and an obvious violation of the WHO/UNICEF 1981 code on marketing of breast milk substitutes.

Once the baby has started sucking he should be given the breast on demand. Usually the mother and the child will after some days develop a fairly regular schedule. The child will cry for the breast whenever the stomach is empty, which is usually 2-3 hours after a meal. This is about the time needed for the breasts to be filled. When put to the breast the baby will finish most of the contents within 10 minutes.

If the breast-feeding runs smoothly additional food is not required until the baby is 4-6 months old and breast-feeding should be continued, preferably for at least 2 years.

Breast-feeding problems

Fissures in the nipple may occur, especially if the baby is sucking in a wrong way. The mother may need assistance in order to correct the position. Some milk should be left on the nipples after every feeding (in order to enhance the healing) and the breast should be exposed to air and sun.

When the milk flows to the breasts on the second to third day the breasts may be congested, painful and the mother may develop a transient fever. Keep the breasts warm, try to empty them and give some aspirin for pain relief.

If reddening and swelling of the breast occurs the breasts should be emptied as carefully as possible. There is no reason not to let the infant suck. If the mother does not want to breast-feed she will have to express the milk by hand. Keep the breasts warm. If the pain is severe aspirin is recommended. If a mastitis is developing antibiotics should be given and if an abscess develops the mother should be referred for incision.

If the infant is too weak to suck (e.g. due to disease or immaturity) the milk should be expressed and given to the baby by spoon or a cup.

Maternal health education

Before leaving the health unit after delivery women should be given adequate information on puerperal hygiene, breast-feeding, family planning (see Appendix VI) and care of the newborn. Such health education is mandatory to maintain the health of the mother and to motivate her to return for post-natal check-ups for herself and the newborn.

Involving the father

It is increasingly clear that any improvement in the reproductive health of women is completely dependent on the interest and the involvement of the husband. His co-operation right from the early puerperium is vital for good neonatal and maternal health. All experience indicates that the involvement of the father must be initiated during pregnancy. The indifferent husband will not pay sufficient attention to his wife either at delivery, or after it.

FURTHER READING

1.

Savage King, F. *Helping Mothers to Breast Feed*. Revised edition African Medical and Research Foundation (AMREF): Nairobi, 1992.

REFERENCES

1. UNICEF. The innocenti declaration. Statement from a meeting in Florence, 1990.

2. Victoria, C.G., Smith, P.G., Vaughan, J.P. *et al*. Evidence for protection of breast feeding against infant deaths from infectious diseases in Brazil. *The Lancet* 1987; ii: 319-22.

6

The Complicated Pregnancy

A variety of medical complications may appear during pregnancy, delivery and puerperium. A woman who starts her pregnancy in poor health runs a higher risk of complications, and if she is living under difficult circumstances with little or no access to health care, the danger of a fatal ending for the baby and/or herself may be high. Thus, in the developing world, a combination of several unfavourable external circumstances often leads to several medical pregnancy complications in the same woman, contributing to a poor outcome.

Anaemia

Importance and definition

World-wide, anaemia is one of the most common complications of pregnancy. Between 25 and 50 per cent of all pregnant woman in developing countries are anaemic. If serious and left untreated this may threaten the life of fetus and mother. It also contributes significantly to maternal morbidity during pregnancy, and to loss of maternal productivity.

Anaemia during pregnancy is defined by WHO as a haemoglobin concentration of 110 g/litre or less. Many pregnant women with haemoglobin around 110 g/litre are apparently healthy, however, so perhaps the limit should be 100 g/litre or for a haematocrit (or packed cell volume, PCV) of 30 per cent or less. In clinical practice a rapid but careful inspection of the conjunctival, inner surface of the lower eye-lid will detect the majority of anaemic women. If the woman has an eye infection, or has eyes irritated by smoke from cooking, the paleness of the tongue and palms assists in detecting anaemia.

Causes

The most important causes of pregnancy anaemia are iron deficiency, folic acid deficiency, malaria or other infections, and hereditary haemoglobin deficiencies.

IRON DEFICIENCY   Iron deficiency occurs as a result of the extra iron demands of the growing fetus and the increasing maternal blood volume which are not met by dietary intake. Often the woman has even started her pregnancy with an iron deficiency, either as an isolated problem or as a component of general malnutrition, and without extra attention this iron deficiency will invariably increase during pregnancy. Many women also lose iron through intestinal parasites, especially **hookworm.**

FOLIC ACID DEFICIENCY   Folic acid is, like iron, a critical substance for production of red blood cells. In fact it is needed for construction of all new cells, including the growth of the fetus. Folic acid or folate is mainly found in green leaves and other green vegetables. It is destroyed by long cooking. One disease that destroys many cells, demanding an increased production of new cells and thereby increasing the need for folate intake, is malaria.

MALARIA   Malaria resistance decreases during pregnancy in otherwise semi-immune women in holo-endemic malaria areas (i.e., areas were malaria transmission occurs throughout the year) and the pregnant woman will suffer more frequently from malaria attacks. Such attacks lead to the destruction of red blood cells, causing anaemia and folate deficiency, and also to a bone marrow depression which further contributes to pregnancy anaemia. Malaria is discussed further in the section on Infections (see page 125).

HEREDITARY HAEMOGLOBIN DEFECTS   These are the one cause of pregnancy anaemia that is impossible to prevent. Sickle cell disease is widely prevalent in Africa, and thalassaemia is common in the Mediterranean area. Both cause mainly haemolytic anaemia, destroying red blood cells, though folate deficiency and infections may contribute to the anaemia.

Effects

Common symptoms of light or moderate anaemia are fatigue, shortness of breath, dizziness and headache. Oedema of the legs is common. When the anaemia becomes more severe fatigue increases, but it is still remarkable how a woman with extreme degrees of chronic anaemia may walk about pursuing her daily tasks. With haemoglobin levels below 60 or 70 g/litre the fetus is no longer adequately oxygenated, however, and there is an increased risk of fetal or infant loss. At such levels of anaemia the woman has tachycardia, and venous pulsations are visible on the neck. With severe chronic anaemia even a moderate or small haemorrhage during delivery may kill the mother. She is also susceptible to infections, particularly in the puerperium, and combined chronic anaemia, intrapartum haemorrhage and puerperal sepsis is a common cause of maternal death.

Prevention

Adequate nutrition is often difficult to achieve for the impoverished pregnant woman in many developing countries. An extra intake of iron in tablet form plus possible routine hookworm treatment during pregnancy will improve iron balance. Health education stressing the intake of green leaves will hopefully improve folate intake. Many antenatal care programmes in developing countries include malaria suppression as routine.

Management

When anaemia is clinically evident, treatment must be more aggressive, and one very important component of antenatal care is therefore screening for anaemia. Moderate anaemia may be treated on an out-patient basis with iron (ferrous sulphate is cheapest), with malaria suppression, hookworm treatment and folates. The patient will not be able to handle all these drugs at once and close follow-up is thus mandatory. Clinical search for other infections such as tuberculosis, HIV etc. is important. Serious anaemia with signs of cardiac incompensation should be treated in hospital with careful monitoring of the progressive treatment, which may include digoxin, transfusions of packed blood, antimalarials and possibly antibiotics. When the anaemic woman presents at birth, it is important to minimise blood loss and to start treatment along the above lines at once in the puerperium.

Malnutrition

The most common form of malnutrition encountered in pregnant women in the third world is general protein – calorie malnutrition, which is the result of a chronic lack of food. The specific deficiencies of iron and folate have been discussed above, and the lack of iodine sometimes encountered in inland areas is also specific.

Diagnosis of general malnutrition

Clinical inspection reveals a thin woman with little subcutaneous fat. She is likely to have had a low pre-pregnant weight, had this been noted. Her weight increase per month during pregnancy will be low. A practical way to screen for general malnutrition is the mid-upper-arm circumference as described on page 16. Often the malnourished woman also has iron deficiency and atrophic signs and/or infections of the tongue and lips. Leg oedema is common.

Effects

General lack of nutrients in the mother will hamper fetal growth, and the baby will often be small for its gestational age at birth. The baby will also often be born with impaired immune defence mechanisms. An isolated protein-calorie malnutrition in an otherwise healthy mother leads to an average fetal weight reduction of up to 500 g, as seen in Europe during the Second World War. In the developing world today general malnutrition of the mother is frequently combined, however, with other elements of a difficult socio-economic situation. For instance, infections are common, particularly sexually transmitted diseases, malaria, tuberculosis and intestinal infections. Such infections contribute to poor health of the mother and child. Maternal anaemia is often seen. Pre-term delivery will be common, and an increase in the perinatal death rate will also be encountered. However, with starvation, the woman is often infertile because ovulation stops.

Management

An optimal diet is often not easy to arrange. If a food supplementation programme is being discussed, pregnant and lactating women should, however, have priority along with small children. A daily supplementation of 430 kcal (1806 kJ), in a groundnut-enriched biscuit and vitaminised tea, to pregnant women studied in Gambia[1] increased mean birth weight by 220 g, and reduced the proportion of babies with birth weights of 2500 g or less from 28 per cent to 4.7 per cent. Another important component of management is the treatment of infections, improving the woman's general condition and resistance. A third component is health education, covering what to eat to improve nutritional status. The information given will depend on the foodstuffs available and affordable in the area, and discussions may also include local food taboos for pregnant women. Finally, a reduced work load will improve the woman's nutritional status by decreasing energy expenditure. More rest at the end of pregnancy is not an easy matter in many societies, however, and in serious cases the husband should be called in and informed about the necessity for rest. It may be important that health services point out the vulnerability of the malnourished woman, both to her husband and family. She may otherwise be one of the last to eat at meal-times.

Hypertensive disorders

Hypertension during pregnancy is commonly defined as a systolic blood pressure > 140 mmHg or a diastolic pressure > 90 mmHg. Where information on blood pressure from early pregnancy is available, a systolic rise of > 30 mmHg or a diastolic rise > 15 mmHg is a better definition. Hypertension during pregnancy may be divided into the following categories: pre-pregnant hypertensive disease, non-proteinuric pregnancy-induced hypertension, pre-eclampsia, and combinations of these.

Pre-pregnancy hypertensive disease

This is defined as hypertension before pregnancy, e.g. because of renal disease or of unknown origin. If possible, women with this disease should be investigated for renal complications, including check of urinary infection and bilharzia. Pre-pregnancy hypertension often becomes more severe during pregnancy and may cause intrauterine growth retardation. It may also develop into pre-eclampsia.

Non-proteinuric pregnancy-induced hypertension

This is defined as hypertension developed during pregnancy but without signs of pre-eclampsia. This condition often later develops into pre-eclampsia. As long as the urine contains no protein the condition may be monitored on an out-patient basis with a thorough check-up once or twice weekly.

Pre-eclampsia (toxemia)

This is a syndrome of unknown origin that may develop in the third trimester. It is characterised by hypertension, proteinuria and oedema. As oedema is very common in normal pregnancy it is in fact an unreliable sign of pre-eclampsia. Pre-eclampsia, once developed, will continue to the end of pregnancy.

It often worsens, with rising blood pressure, increasing proteinuria and such symptoms as nausea, vomiting, headache and unclear vision. When symptoms like these develop the risk of eclampsia (convulsions and loss of consciousness) is great.

Eclampsia is associated with high maternal and fetal mortality and is in fact one of the 'big maternal killers' in many developing countries.

Management

Detection of pre-eclampsia is important, in order to avoid eclampsia. If possible, routine blood pressure measurements should be performed at all last trimester antenatal visits. In cases of raised blood pressure or suspicious symptoms (headache, nausea etc) urine analysis should be performed. Heavy proteinuria, or recently developed proteinuria, strengthens the diagnosis of pre-eclampsia. Women with pre-eclampsia should rest in hospital and be delivered if the complication is becoming more severe. Severe pre-eclampsia and eclampsia are treated with intravenous magnesium sulphate to prevent or stop convulsions (see Chapter 7).

The **out-patient** treatment of pregnant women with hypertension should ideally imply frequent (once or twice a week) checks of blood pressure and proteinuria. It is **highly questionable** whether anti-hypertensive treatment would be recommendable in **out-patient** antenatal care. Pregnancy hypertension will continue to threaten the fetus and the woman until delivery. In case of severe hypertension (e.g. blood pressure > 160/110 mmHg and tendency to increase), particularly with simultaneous proteinuria (+ + or + + +), **induction of labour** with oxytocin should be considered.

The problem of **out-patient** treatment of pregnancy hypertension is that a 1-week prescription of a peroral drug may give the pregnant woman the (false) impression that the disease is 'cured', which, of course, is not the case. The correct management should, therefore, be very restrictive in prescribing drugs but rather encourage **rest and frequent checks** (once or twice a week). A certificate, describing the seriousness of the disease and the need for rest, signed by the senior staff involved, should be **directed to the husband** and given to the woman.

In those women whose disease motivates **in-patient** care antihypertensive treatment may be given as a **pre-delivery** measure. Care should, however, be taken not to reduce the blood pressure too drastically, since it may harm the fetus. Oral treatment with hydralazine can be given in a dose of 25-50 mg three to four times daily. In acutely and severely hypertensive patients dihydrolizine 6.25-12.50 mg may be given intramuscularly in repeated doses.

Pre-term labour

Epidemiology

Over two-thirds of all infant deaths during the first week after birth occur in low birth-weight babies. Some of them are born pre-term with weight adequate for gestational age (AGA). Both AGA and small for gestational age (SGA) newborns can thus be born in the pre-term (or in the term) period. The problem of low birth-weight babies is thus very large in the developing world, and such perinatal losses are in fact losses to the national economy and productivity.

Causes

Socio-economic factors contribute greatly to pre-term labour and to intrauterine growth retardation. A low socio-economic level is reflected in a variety of ways: lack of clean water, malnutrition, sexually transmitted diseases and other infections, too frequent pregnancies, heavy physical work throughout pregnancy, and lack of antenatal/delivery care.

Infections of the vagina and cervix may be the direct agent of pre-term delivery, as described in the section on infections (page 123). Febrile infections may also cause pre-term contractions. Malaria causes anaemia, fever and placental insufficiency and may give rise to pre-term birth. Practically all factors that can cause intrauterine growth retardation, can also cause pre-term delivery. Thus a high proportion of low birth-weight babies (< 2500 g) in a community is an indicator of underdevelopment. The problem should ideally be solved through development in general, and improvement of the condition of women in particular.

Management

The diagnosis of pre-term labour evidently depends on a reasonably correct estimation of gestational age. If many weeks remain until term, and the woman reports a distinct increase in uterine contractions, longer duration of contractions, painful contractions, and periods of regular contractions, this is a cause for concern. Careful questioning can often distinguish these symptoms of **imminent pre-term labour** from the normal irregular contractions that gradually increase during any normal pregnancy. Low pelvic pressure and lower back pain strengthen the likelihood of imminent pre-term labour in women with suspicious patterns of uterine contractions.

If a careful vaginal examination confirms cervical ripening or cervical dilatation the woman should be given bedrest either at home (a note should be sent to the husband or employer) or in a maternity hostel (to ensure sexual abstinence). If the cervical opening/dilatation is far advanced and the pregnancy is very pre-term, the woman is best treated in hospital.

Established pre-term labour with regular contractions, dilatation and effacement of the cervix can be treated in hospital by the injection or infusion of tocolytic drugs (terbutaline, salbutamol and other drugs that counteract uterine contractions) but in most cases the effect is doubtful. Ideally these drugs may postpone a pre-term birth for 24-48 hours, a time period that may permit accelerated lung maturation in the fetus. The start of labour means the start of rapid maturation of the lungs, though this process takes 24-48 hours. Rapid pre-term birth (hours) does not give time for such lung maturation; and the pre-term baby will have a higher risk of 'hyaline membrane disease', also called respiratory distress syndrome than with a postponement of 24-48 hours. It is not normally possible to postpone active pre-term labour for more than a day or two.

It is extremely important for the obstetric staff to remember that the pre-term fetus is very sensitive to **asphyxia, infection,** and **prolonged labour**. The chances of survival will depend to a large extent on its condition at birth.

Prelabour rupture of the membranes pre-term

Prelabour rupture of the membranes pre-term is defined as ruptured membranes without contractions before 37 completed weeks of pregnancy. This condition was often previously called premature rupture of the membranes.

Management

Women with this condition should be admitted to hospital due to the high perinatal risks. The risk at a particular gestational age will depend a great deal on the paediatric resources available. At a gestational age where the perinatal risk of delivery is very high, an expectant attitude may be wise, with daily temperature checks. **Tocolytic drugs should not be given.** Once an intrauterine infection is suspected, labour should be induced, and antibiotics given for protection.

Intrauterine growth retardation

The most common causes of intrauterine growth retardation (IUGR) are infections, above all malaria, maternal hypertension and smoking, though a variety of causes exist. Malaria suppression is therefore an important prophylactic measure. The cheapest way to detect IUGR is by measuring the symphysis – fundus distance. By frequent retraining of midwives in the correct and meticulous use of a tape measure at all antenatal visits a valuable set of symphysis – fundus measurements will be produced allowing early recognition of inadequate fetal growth and possible IUGR (see Figure 25).

Management

Active management should include **fetal movement registration** by the mother. A rule of thumb may be to require at least 10 fetal movements from sunrise to noon. Serious IUGR should lead to in-patient care and induction of labour or Caesarean section.

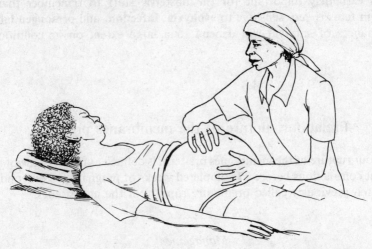

Figure 21   Detection of breech presentations is important during late third
trimester antenatal visit. In detected cases either pre-delivery
external version, or hospital delivery with trained staff present
should take place.

Breech presentation

Breech delivery in inexperienced hands is associated with a very high mortality
rate and is a common situation in developing countries. It is therefore essential
to detect a breech presentation before delivery by careful palpation of the fetus,
and midwives must be trained to perform such a diagnosis (Figure 21).

Management

Once diagnosed in the last month of pregnancy, the midwife must refer the
mother for **external version** or delivery at a unit where staff are experienced
in such procedures. External version is described in Figure 22. If external version
is not performed it is imperative that the mother gives birth in a health unit
with well trained staff, experienced in assisting in a breech delivery.

Twins

Twin pregnancies are common in the third world. One of the highest prevalence
figures described has been reported from Nigeria, 4.6 per cent, while Japan
shows figures around 0.6 per cent. A multiple pregnancy may be suspected with a
high symphysis – fundus distance, and often confirmed at palpation and/or
auscultation ('Three or more large fetal parts').

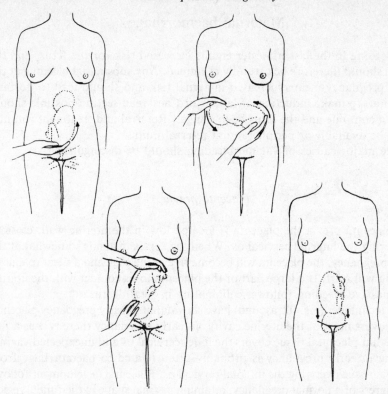

Figure 22 External version of breech presentation. If no contraindications (haemorrhage, pre-eclampsia, growth retardation or other) are present, and fetal heart sounds are checked before, during and after version, this is a safe procedure that should be performed from around the 37th week. Intravenous tocolysis is very helpful. The **first** step is to lift the fetal pelvis upward. The **second** step is to carefully support the downward movement of the fetal head and simultaneously lifting the fetal pelvis. The **third** step is to pass the transverse position coming to oblique position. The **fourth** step is ensuring that the fetal head is in the pelvic inlet. External version is performed by one person only and must never be painful to the mother. Note: External version is performed with the mother lying down.

Management

Multiple pregnancy increases nutritional demands on the mother, and anti-anaemics should be given. To prevent premature delivery the mother and father must be made to understand the importance of less work for the mother. A typed note to the employer may even be necessary on occasions. Threat of pre-term labour should, where possible, lead to bed rest at a health unit. Delivery should take place at a referral unit with experienced staff.

Maternal haemorrhage

Any bleeding in the last trimester entails increased risk for the fetus, and the woman should therefore be carefully examined. Any substantial bleeding at the end of pregnancy means increased maternal risk and should lead to hospital admission, to make induction of labour or Caesarean section possible should bleeding continue and the fetus be in danger. Referral and treatment routines should be available at peripheral and referral units.

Three major causes of vaginal bleeding should be distinguished.

Placenta previa

With placenta previa the placenta is located low in the uterine wall, close to or covering the internal cervical os. When the cervix distends somewhat at the end of pregnancy, the placenta will become free at the edge and a silent (painless) bleeding will start. If a large part of the placenta loses contact with the uterine wall, massive bleeding follows, culminating in fetal death.

New techniques (e.g. ultrasound) have shown that in early pregnancy placental tissue covers most of the uterine cavity. In early pregnancy there is thus a fair chance that placental tissue covers the inner cervical os and unexpected vaginal bleeding in early pregnancy is probably often related to haemorrhage from placental tissue overlying the internal cervical os. Placental development follows the progress of a normal pregnancy, attaining its final shape in the fundal region or on the uterine walls away from the internal os of the cervix. Only about 1 per cent of all pregnant women have placental tissue overlying the internal cervical os at term. The head (or breech) is typically non-engaged in such cases.

MANAGEMENT   Management consists of strict bed rest after diagnosis by very careful vaginal examination, preferably in the operating room (massive haemorrhage may occur!) and Caesarean section delivery.

Placental abruption

Placental abruption is detachment of the normally located placenta. The resultant haemorrhage between the placenta and the uterine wall causes pain, and tenderness over the uterus.

If a large part (more than a quarter to a third) of the placenta detaches, fetal distress and fetal death may occur.

MANAGEMENT   Management consists of strict bed rest after diagnosis and artificial rupture of the membranes, close check on fetal heart during vaginal delivery, and Caesarean section, where necessary.

In both cases – placenta previa and placental abruption – an intravenous drip is advisable, blood transfusion should be given where necessary, and, available, injectable aminokaproic acid to enhance clotting.

It should be noted that abruption may be complicated by coagulation disorders.

Placenta previa and placental abruption are discussed in greater detail in Chapter 7.

Diseases of the uterine cervix

It is important to remember that vaginal bleeding during pregnancy may originate from the cervix. Cervical cancer is much more common in poorer than in rich countries.

MANAGEMENT   Management should be expectant. Careful inspection of the portio is indispensable in all kinds of vaginal bleeding, as well as during pregnancy. A number of benign lesions include polyps and inflammatory conditions of the cervix and vagina. Cervical bleeding that does not stop spontaneously or has a duration of months should be observed by a doctor in order to attempt to exclude malignancy. Management should include treatment of any vaginitis present. Local treatment of the cervix is not advisable unless malignancy has been excluded.

Abdominal pregnancy

In countries with widespread tubal disease due to sexually transmitted diseases, ectopic pregnancies are common. Such ectopic pregnancies may even progress to a stage in which the fetus is viable and constitute a problem at delivery. Such **abdominal pregnancies** may occur as adnexal (often ovarian) pregnancies.

Abdominal pregnancies are often detected very late and they almost always have an unstable or transverse fetal lie which is impossible to correct by external version/manipulation. Sometimes they may even occur as postdate pregnancies and are impossible to induce. At any time suspected cases should be sent to a well-equipped hospital. Injection of a radio-opaque solution into the cervix will make X-ray diagnosis possible since the uterine cavity will be outlined in anatomical relation to the fetus. Such a measure will not harm the fetus and will give the correct diagnosis quickly if X-ray equipment is available.

Management

Management consists always of laparotomy and extraction of the fetus. The bulk of these cases will not give a viable fetus and the risk of stillbirth is great.

Intrauterine fetal death

Causes

The most common causes of intrauterine fetal death before the start of labour are syphilis, other infections, pre-eclampsia and intrauterine growth retardation. To these are added the ascending infections after membrane rupture (many women do not or cannot seek medical care if the membranes have ruptured and there are no contractions) and delivery complications such as asphyxia, malpositioning, uterine rupture, cord complications etc.

Management

The clinical condition of the mother is much better in a case of intrauterine fetal death due to syphilis in an otherwise healthy woman than in a case of fetal death due to a delivery catastrophe. Thus, the condition of the woman must determine the treatment. Dehydration, anaemia, oliguria, sepsis, malaria must be treated urgently if the woman is severely ill. If the membranes are broken, she must be delivered when her general condition has been brought under control. A woman with a normal general condition apart from absence of fetal heart sounds does not, however, constitute an obstetrical emergency. An expectant attitude is advisable in such cases, and the mother may return home.

Coagulation disorders and tendency to bleeding as an effect of a retained fetus are rare, and occur only after a long period after fetal death. Delivery of the dead fetus is described in Chapter 7.

FURTHER READING

Chalmers, I., Enkin, M., Keirse, M.J.N.C. *Effective Care in Pregnancy and Childbirth. Volume I: Pregnancy.* Oxford University Press: Oxford, 1989.

REFERENCE

1. Prentice, M.L., Whitehead, R.G., Watkinson, M. *et al.* Prenatal dietary supplementation of African women and birth weight. *Lancet* 1983; **i:** 489-92.

7

The Complicated Birth

Possible prevention of delivery complications depends on an early recognition of discrete signs of obstetrical danger. In an environment at home or in a busy health unit, non-alarming but clinically highly relevant symptoms may escape attention. Such symptoms may include blurred consciousness or confusion (incipient eclampsia), slight vaginal bleeding and otherwise silent umbilical cord complications.

Protracted delivery (dystocia)

'Dystocia' (literally difficult labour) will in this context refer merely to cephalic presentations. Other fetal presentations will be treated separately.

It is clinically important to make a distinction between the two kinds of protracted delivery, mechanical and dynamic dystocia. All forms of protracted labour can be classified according to either of these two categories, though both categories may exist simultaneously.

Mechanical dystocia

Mechanical dystocia is identical to obstructed labour. The obstruction might be due to either **the fetus** (large or malformed fetus, cephalic) or **the mother** (narrow pelvic canal, deficient pelvic growth, pelvic bones deformed by a previous injury or soft tissue tumour such as myoma or pelvic kidney or scarred vulva due to genital mutilation).

There is no widely accepted definition of mechanical dystocia. From a practical point of view it would be sufficient to say that mechanical dystocia in the **active phase** of dilatation exists when cervical dilatation has reached at least 4 cm without any progress during a 2-hour period of adequate labour (see Chapter 3).

This definition is clinically sensitive in that it guarantees **early recognition** of dystocia. It should be regarded as a definition aiming more at alarm than at intervention. It aims at avoiding undue delay in the recognition of a partogram deviation and further aims at helping to differentiate the two categories of dystocia – mechanical and dynamic.

The definition of mechanical dystocia in the **expulsion phase** should be failure to make progress during more than 1 hour of adequate labour and sufficient maternal expulsion force. If the fetal heart rate and the general condition of the mother do not give cause for alarm, intervention can be delayed until 2 hours have passed after diagnosis.

Complications of unrecognised mechanical dystocia may cause **ischaemia** in the anterior portion of the uterine isthmus and in the bladder (due to tissue compression between fetal skull and back of symphysis), leading to tissue necrosis, infections and finally, **fistulas.**

Nerve damage due to compression of branches of the sciatic nerve might lead to chronic neurological sequelae (drop foot).

Uterine rupture is one of the most feared complications with mechanical dystocia in a multipara. An early sign is the so-called Bandl's furrow (see Figure 23). Uterine rupture is a particular risk in women with **previous Caesarean section** and in **grand multiparae**. Sudden vaginal bleeding with pre-existing clinical signs of mechanical dystocia should alert the staff.

MANAGEMENT   There are only two solutions to verified **mechanical dystocia during active dilatation of the cervix: symphysiotomy** or **Caesarean section** (see Appendices for details). The cervicogram (partogram) routine (see

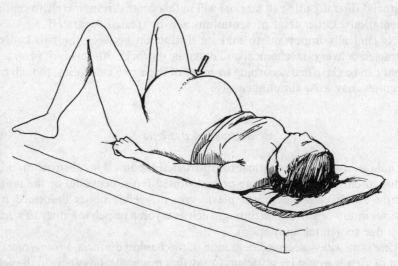

Figure 23   In cases of obstructed labour the lowermost portion of the uterus – the isthmus – is distended and a furrow ('Bandl's furrow') demarcates the isthmus from the rest of the uterine corpus.

Chapter 3) should be followed, with due attention paid to the contraction pattern. The usual rotation and flexion of the fetal head may have been disturbed, resulting in face or brow presentation or malposition of the fetal head above the pelvic brim. In addition to typical signs of partogram deviation there are several other signs that may confirm the diagnosis of mechanical dystocia. Various degrees of moulding of the fetal head from palpable scalp oedema to compression of the fetal parietal bones or deformation of the fetal head indicate various degrees of cephalopelvic disproportion. Vulvar oedema may be an external sign of voluntary maternal efforts to force the fetus past the pelvic canal.

Mechanical dystocia in the expulsion phase may be difficult to distinguish from dynamic dystocia and/or failure to progress due to maternal exhaustion. There are no simple means for verifying the diagnosis apart from tentative extraction by vacuum extraction (VE) or by forceps (see Appendix I for details). Such 'trial of VE' will give information as to whether or not the fetal head is following downwards in the birth canal by simultaneous maternal expulsion effort (during contractions) and extraction effort. If there is no progress and the head is positioned in such a way as to allow for symphysiotomy, such intervention is called for (see Appendix II for details).

The clinical management required in cases of mechanical dystocia depends on the prognosis for the mother and for the fetus. In situations where life is threatened the mother's life should always be given higher precedence than the life of the fetus. **Caesarean section should be avoided at any price when the fetus is dead, unless it is necessary for the sake of the mother.** The doctor should have experience of destructive fetal operations. The guiding principle should be to minimise surgical trauma. Caesarean section should also be avoided when there is a grossly malformed fetus verified, unless operation is required for maternal reasons.

Dynamic dystocia

Dynamic dystocia is equivalent to insufficient uterine contractions during labour. It occurs frequently in parturients in poor general condition with dehydration, malnutrition and infections. The result is a protracted delivery.

Dynamic dystocia is a **symptom** either of adverse general living conditions or of a hidden obstetrical problem, e.g. a pre-existent mechanical dystocia. The **'exhausted uterus'** should therefore always be approached with utmost care, since it may be a uterus prone to rupture due to hidden disproportion, malposition or other obstetric complication incompatible with vaginal delivery.

MANAGEMENT   The first task for the midwife is to attempt to **exclude** an underlying **mechanical dystocia**. Do past obstetric history (previous problems), current pregnancy data (large fetus) or clinical signs (scalp oedema, moulding of fetal head) suggest overlooked mechanical dystocia? Does manual assessment of pelvic size indicate disproportion? While clarifying the above an attempt should be made to correct any metabolic deviation disturbing uterine contractions. If the history and current clinical picture do not indicate imminent obstetric disaster, artificial rupture of the membranes or **a careful trial of oxytocin stimulation may be attempted.**

Oxytocin is a very potent drug and is frequently given in too large doses. It should therefore be used with **utmost care**. If a woman with dynamic dystocia is given oxytocin by infusion the initial dosage should be small. Distinguish between multiparae and nulliparae:

In **multiparae** it is advisable to start with a concentration of 2.5 units of oxytocin/litre and an initial drop rate of 15 per minute. The drop rate should be doubled every 30 minutes until the first contractions have been registered by abdominal palpation. Care should be taken not to increase the dosage without close supervision. Such patients should never be left for more than 30 minutes without observation, since uterine rupture may even occur with only slight overstimulation.

In **nulliparae** the risk of uterine rupture is almost nil. A higher initial dosage is advisable (5 units/litre) though the increase in drop rate should be similar (doubling every 30 minutes). The earliest sign of overdosage is fetal bradycardia. Any such sign should lead to immediate interruption of oxytocin administration.

Abnormal fetal presentations

Breech delivery

Breech presentation in **antenatal** care has been treated in Chapter 5. The importance of external version was emphasised and early antenatal recognition of a breech is indispensable for lowering perinatal mortality in this category.

A breech delivery where external version has not been attempted or has failed should be regarded as a high-risk delivery. Where various options (vaginal *versus* abdominal delivery) exist **the following circumstances argue against vaginal delivery:**

1. manual (palpatory) suspicion of feto-pelvic disproportion: large baby or small pelvis

2. previous Caesarean section

3. complicated obstetric history with several fetal/child losses

4. footling presentation (baby presents with straight legs)

5. expected birth-weight below 1500 g and fair chance of neonatal survival

6. signs of intercurrent disease (intrauterine growth retardation, pre-eclampsia, etc).

The management of breech presentations can be characterised by the word obstetrics (Latin obstetrix = to expect in front of). An active though expectant attitude is a prerequisite for optimum management. The risk of dynamic dystocia can be reduced by a prophylactic (early initiation of) oxytocin infusion in the expulsion phase in case of uterine inertia. Frequent auscultation of the fetal heart rate is indispensable due to the risk of umbilical cord complications. Expectant management should continue until most of the fetal body is outside the vulva. **A good rule is never to touch the fetal body until the scapula is visible in the vulva.**

The problem with difficulties in delivering the aftercoming head in breech deliveries was previously solved by the use of forceps. A newer, simpler technique using a bimanual approach via the rectum and via the abdominal wall from above has made the use of forceps in most cases unnecessary (see Figure 24). The intervention is explained in the legend. In more difficult cases **symphysiotomy** is a possible alternative[1,2] (see Appendix III).

Transverse lie at delivery

This complication is most often associated with pre-term delivery. In the pre-term period transverse lie and breech presentation are much more prevalent than in the term period. Abundant amniotic fluid, low-lying placenta, soft tissue tumour (myoma, pelvic kidney or other tumour) may also be a mechanical cause. Genital malformation in the mother, twin pregnancy and abdominal pregnancy may lead to transverse lie of the fetus.

The most feared complication in transverse fetal lie in a woman in labour

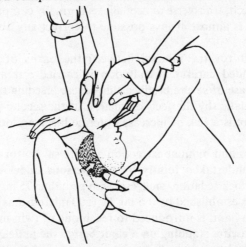

Figure 24　When there are difficulties in delivering the aftercoming head in a breech presentation the midwife's rectal finger along the anterior face of the sacrum may help to get the fetal head free. Note that an assistant should keep the baby's legs upwards, while the midwife's abdominal hand firmly pushes the fetal head downwards.

is early rupture of the membranes. The risk of umbilical cord prolapse is imminent and ensuing strong uterine contractions may make any kind of correction of the lie difficult. It is important to try to exclude placenta previa, soft tissue tumour and other obstacles in the pelvic canal before attempting an external version, preferably utilising tocolytic treatment. The management of a transverse lie during labour without access to Caesarean section must include a decisive attempt to correct the lie by the use of tocolysis, e.g. terbutaline or salbutamol given intravenously using a dose of 0.25 mg (250 micrograms). With the patient in a tilted position (head slightly down, feet slightly up) it is most often possible to achieve a cephalic presentation without cord complication. Management of a prolapsed cord is presented on page 73.

Twin birth

Twin births are associated with increased perinatal mortality and it is therefore advisable to manage twin deliveries as high-risk cases. Twin number two has a much higher mortality rate than that of number one.

Management

Intrapartum separation of the placenta, cord prolapse and protracted delivery are the causes of this increased risk. Provided twin number one is in a longitudinal position (cephalic or breech presentation) and conditions for vaginal delivery prevail, Caesarean section can be avoided. Any position of twin number two, breech, transverse or cephalic, is normally compatible with vaginal delivery, since it is almost always possible to correct any abnormal lie of the second twin.

The time limit for the interval between the births of the twins is not important, provided careful auscultation is carried out after each uterine contraction. In case of severe bradycardia, severe bleeding or other complication, manual podalic (by the feet) extraction of the second twin is advisable. Post-partum there is a risk of increased uterine bleeding, due to atony of the uterine wall.

Podalic version and manual extraction are life-savers for twin number two and should be undertaken **jointly by two persons under the protection of tocolysis**. After quick sedation/analgesia with pethidine 75 mg IV (or equivalent drug), tocolysis is established by 0.5 mg IV (500 micrograms) of terbutaline or salbutamol and a hand is introduced to reach one of twin number two's feet. The assistant midwife, **standing on a chair beside the patient,** places both her palms over the fundus and exerts maximum pressure along the long axis of the uterus. The fundal pressure executed guarantees: 1) flexion of the fetal head and 2) non-extension of fetal arms. Parallel external fundal pressure and fetal extraction downwards under tocolysis and analgesia guarantee best outcome for both mother and the second twin.

Placenta previa

Placenta 'pre-via' (meaning placenta lying in front of the baby) occurs in about 5-10 per thousand deliveries.

Placenta previa is three to four times more common in women above 35 years of age than in women below 35. It is also more frequent with increasing parity.

The diagnosis is recognised by sudden, arterial bleeding from the vagina most often without concomitant uterine contractions or other genital symptoms. Such clinical features are characteristic and distinguish placenta previa from abruptio of the placenta.

Management

All pregnant women suspected of having placenta previa should be guaranteed rest in a horizontal position, causing less tension on the lower uterine segment and less bleeding from the placental site.

Diagnosis is difficult when ultrasound is not available. The clinical course will determine clinical conduct. It should be emphasised that a **manual, vaginal palpation is dangerous**, unless there is immediate access to a surgical theatre equipped for Caesarean section.

The treatment in cases with clinical features of placenta previa is always Caesarean section. In a hospital, immediate surgery may save cases with placenta previa if blood transfusion (or other suitable intravenous fluid) and rapid surgical intervention are within reach. Management of such cases when far away from surgical facilities and where there is profuse vaginal bleeding indicating placenta previa should follow the following steps:

1. A **Trendelenburg position** is most important in order to guarantee high position of legs and uterus and a low head position. The resulting fall in blood pressure will mean less vaginal bleeding in this position, while the cerebral circulation of the mother is at least slightly improved.

2. Any kind of **IV drip** (preferably blood or blood replacement fluid) should be established **through at least two veins.**

If the vaginal bleeding continues in spite of adoption of the Trendelenburg position, the arterial blood pressure will eventually drop and the woman will die from hypovolemic shock. In such a situation there is one final measure left where it is a matter of life or death. Since the blood pressure in the abdominal aorta will gradually drop it is possible to attempt **an outer compression of the abdominal aorta** (despite the presence of a fetus *in utero*) using a method similar to that described below (see page 67). Any kind of cloth or sheet can be used to ensure an external compression of the abdominal wall and the uterus against the abdominal aorta of the woman. During transport a sheet should be very firmly fixed to a stretcher on both sides of the woman in order to attain the desirable compression. Small doses, 25-50 mg, of intravenous pethidine may help the patient to withstand the pain and the discomfort associated with compression of the aorta. Obviously, such compression is extremely uncomfortable and should be exerted as low as possible, preferably over the umbilicus region and always as a **final and last measure** in a dying woman. Compression higher than the umbilicus level will impede respiration and provoke visceral pain. It is technically important to make maximum use of the pregnant uterus as a pillow over the abdominal aorta. Any amount of blood loss prevented is of utmost value in trying to save the life of such women. **A useful criterion of efficient compression is diminishing vaginal bleeding and/or cessation of the arterial pulsation in the patient's groin** (see also page 67).

If cervical opening allows for **extraction of the fetal foot, the fetal leg/pelvis can be utilized as a tamponade** downwards in order to stop uterine bleeding.

Abruptio placentae

Premature detachment of the placenta before the fetus has been expelled can provoke potentially fatal asphyxia for the fetus and intrauterine bleeding for the woman, resulting in possible death. The magnitude of the problem is similar to that of placenta previa and about 1 per cent of pregnancies are complicated by partial or total placental detachment.

There is an increased risk of new abruption of the placenta in forthcoming pregnancies. One abruptio carries an approximately 15 per cent risk of repetition. Two abruptions increase the risk to about 25 per cent.

A placental detachment could be minor or total and **there may be no signs of external bleeding** via the vagina. In such cases there is usually a retroplacental haematoma with gradually developing severe anaemia, pale conjunctivae and most often a tender, hard uterus. In such cases the diagnosis is clear. In less extensive abruption the clinical features are often confusing. Local pain in the uterine wall may indicate local abruptio and should suggest intensive monitoring of blood pressure, fetal heart rate etc.

Should a retroplacental haematoma gradually develop there is an increased risk of coagulation disturbance since coagulation factors are consumed by the haematoma. The risk is particularly high (30 per cent) when the clinical features of abruptio are present and the fetus is dead.

Management

In hospital the treatment depends on the condition of the fetus. If there are no signs of fetal asphyxia and there is no potentially fatal vaginal bleeding, a vaginal delivery may be attempted but there must be immediate access to Caesarean section if needed should signs of fetal distress occur. If the cervix is closed and non-effaced, Caesarean section is advisable. In cases with established fetal death *in utero,* **Caesarean section** is not performed unless laparotomy is deemed absolutely necessary for the mother (intractable, profuse vaginal bleeding). Even a perineotomy can kill a woman with severe abruptio placenta, dead fetus and incipient coagulopathy.

A **simple test of coagulopathy** can be carried out by taking 5 ml of the patient's blood in a clean test tube. After sealing, the tube is placed in the axilla of the patient (or in some other suitable place with body temperature) for 5 minutes. Observation of the test tube after about 5 minutes will, in normal cases, reveal a blood clot. In the case of coagulopathy, completely uncoagulated blood will remain. If there are signs of deficient clotting a blood transfusion, as fresh as possible, should be given.

Should coagulopathy be confirmed **increased fibrinolysis** may be present, causing coagulated blood to be dissolved. A 'model blood clot' obtained from anyone's blood can be mixed with the serum of the patient (after centrifugation), incubated close to 37°C (patient's axilla or other suitable place) and observed after 10 minutes. Any degree of dissolution of the model clot in the patient's serum indicates increased fibrinolysis. In such cases tentative treatment with tranexamic acid 1 gram IV 3-4 times per 24 hours (or other similar anti-fibrinolytic agent) is advisable.

Bleeding from a non-contracted uterus

An atonic uterus after birth may provoke heavy bleeding due to primary inertia, directly related to expulsion of the fetus. Alternatively, insufficient contraction may be due to an overdistended uterus (twin pregnancy, polyhydramnios, etc.) or a concealed infection (chorioamnionitis). Although infection-related bleedings seem to be more resistant to drugs, the vast majority of bleeding cases respond successfully to medical treatment.

Management

Even outside a health unit and with no drugs available much can be done to stop vaginal bleeding after birth. More important than any drug treatment in such cases is compression of the abdominal aorta (Figure 25). The principle is simple: two hands should be used, one held in the groin to check for arterial pulsations, while the fist of the other is carefully held over the umbilicus and slowly lowered towards the anterior side of the vertebral column. When the arterial pulsations in the groin have vanished the aortic compression is sufficient and vaginal bleeding will cease. This measure is, unfortunately, often forgotten in the hectic conduct of cases of post-partum bleeding. It must be carefully practised in advance in order to prepare the staff to carry out adequate manoeuvres.

Drug treatment of profuse post-partum bleeding in a health unit comprises: oxytocin (10 units IV with repeated doses IV) or ergometrine (0.5 mg)

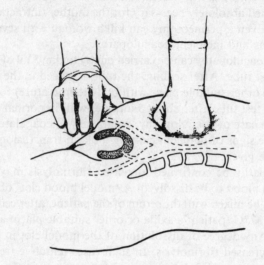

Figure 25   Manual compression of the aorta should be accompanied by palpation of the pulse of the groin (see text)

injection IV, which normally gives sufficient uterine contraction to diminish the haemorrhage. The bladder should be emptied.

In cases that do not respond to these drugs, compression of the abdominal aorta should be carried out. In developed countries prostin F2 alpha (dinoprost) is used. This expensive drug is more powerful and usually results in prompt uterine contraction and haemostasis.

Bleeding from traumatic lacerations

Delivery trauma affects principally four different levels in the delivery canal: corpus, cervix, vagina and vulva/perineum.

Small **lacerations in the corpus uteri** are probably often concealed and will heal spontaneously. Repeated subclinical lacerations may be of clinical importance, since advanced multiparity is known to increase the risk of uterine rupture. The dramatic **rupture of the uterus** is the final stage of a laceration of the uterine corpus. It is usually an anterior laceration with lateral extension, though a rupture may also occur in the posterior wall and even in the fundus region. Careless use of oxytocic drugs often substantially contributes to the majority of rupture cases. Utmost care must be shown when using oxytocic drugs, particularly in multiparous women (see page 62).

Another cause of uterine rupture is careless fundal pressure when using the forearm in the case of uterine inertia or careless fundal pressure during podalic extraction of the second twin (see page 64).

Any fundal pressure is contraindicated unless the cervix is fully dilated.
Lacerations in the cervix uteri are detected by a slow but continuous arterial bleeding from the vagina post-partum. They are most often repaired without problem from below. A high cervical laceration may be continuous with a low corpus laceration and even with a small uterine rupture, however. In doubtful cases, laparotomy is always recommended, particularly since the ureters are dangerously close to the cervix.

Vaginal lacerations are often accessible for repair vaginally, though deep traumas may give severe paravaginal haematomas, sometimes extending upwards in the retroperitoneal space. Such hidden haematomas must be looked for, particularly when there is a sudden drop in blood pressure with a concomitant 'normal' vaginal bleeding. Careful bimanual palpation of the paravaginal region is indispensable. If the patient's circulation is affected (pre-shock or shock), rapid localisation of the bleeding vessel is important. At the same time outer abdominal compression of the aorta (see page 67) is helpful. Vaginal or abdominal repair is advisable depending on the level of the laceration.

Hypertension

Both pregnancy-induced hypertension and pre-existing, essential hypertension can cause delivery complications. The former may give rise to severe pre-eclampsia/eclampsia, while the latter may cause abruptio of the placenta.

Pre-eclampsia/eclampsia is still an enigmatic disease (eclampsia is described in more detail on page 70). Pre-eclampsia is defined as a complication of pregnancy, in which proteinuria is accompanied by an increase in blood pressure above 140/90 mmHg or a pressure increase of 30 mmHg, or more, on the systolic; or 15 mmHg, or more, on the diastolic as recorded before or during early pregnancy. Proteinuria is regarded as an expression of impaired renal function due to renal vasoconstriction and hypoperfusion. Severe pre-eclampsia will lead to exaggerated peripheral tendon reflexes (hyperreflexia), a sign useful in clinical practice (see page 71).

Management

The most important curative aspect of pre-eclampsia is that the disease will continue to threaten the health of the pregnant woman and her fetus until delivery is accomplished. This means that in severe cases clinical management should aim at terminating the pregnancy. Both the mother and the fetus will face increasing risks of impaired health and possibly death by a conservative attitude.

Medical treatment of pre-eclampsia includes antihypertensive drugs such as oral hydralazine or parenteral dihydrolizine. The oral dose may be up to 25-50 mg, four times daily. The parenteral treatment should be given in IM doses of 6.25-12.50 mg. Diazepam will affect the fetus (since it crosses the placenta) but may control hyperreflexia and to some extent hypertension. In severe cases magnesium sulphate should be considered (see below) once delivery has been decided upon.

Delivery is most often successful vaginally and the uterus tends to respond well to oxytocic induction, since it is more reactive to stimuli than the normal uterus. Careful auscultation of the fetal heart rate (always directly after a contraction has passed) is important since pre-eclampsia tends to impair placental function as a result of vasoconstriction and reduced blood flow.

Unconsciousness/convulsions

Loss of consciousness and/or convulsions are often associated with eclampsia. Even if eclampsia is an important cause in such cases, other common disorders may give a similar clinical picture, e.g. cerebral malaria, meningitis and cerebrovascular complications.

Eclampsia

Eclampsia is defined as convulsions with simultaneous symptoms of pre-eclampsia (and absence of a history of epilepsy). Pregnancy-associated elevation of the blood pressure is more important than a current blood pressure value alone. In many impoverished countries, e.g. in Africa, blood pressures are habitually low, often as low as 90/50 mmHg. A systolic elevation of 30 mmHg or a diastolic elevation of 15 mmHg or more is pathological. This means that a blood pressure of 130/80 mmHg is perfectly compatible with full-blown eclampsia.

MANAGEMENT   An unconscious pregnant woman with or without convulsions should immediately be suspected of having eclampsia and be referred to a hospital. Other infectious (cerebral malaria, meningitis) or vascular (cerebral haemorrhage, embolism) diseases should, however, be looked for after initial anti-convulsive treatment. The maternal risk is above all **vomiting and aspiration. A supine lateral position** is indispensable in preventing this complication. Loosely attaching the hands to the bedside is both reasonable and advisable to maintain the lateral position. An indwelling **urinary catheter** must be used both to guarantee emptying of the bladder and to monitor urine production.

Medical treatment of eclampsia should be focused on the **convulsions**. A convenient and safe drug is **magnesium sulphate** ($MgSO_4$), which is given with an initial dose of 5 grams slowly IV in a twice diluted 25 per cent solution for a period of several minutes. This 'bolus dose' of 5 grams should be followed immediately by 5 grams IM. The repeat dose should be 5 grams every 4 hours. The IM routine requires a concentrated MgSO₄ (50 per cent) solution; otherwise too large volumes must be used. Magnesium treatment is uncomplicated and efficient in the treatment of convulsions. There are no serum concentrations to be measured and the clinical effect of magnesium can be monitored in three ways by 2-hourly checks of:

● patellar reflexes

● urinary output

● respiration frequency.

Hyperreflexia should be checked before the treatment is initiated, preferably by **testing knee jerks**. This test, which is not carried out with a 'reflex hammer' but with the **fingertips**, is **repeated every 2 hours** to check for diminished reflexes. If knee jerk activity is found to be strongly diminished or absent, magnesium treatment is stopped. There is no danger in this but **areflexia** is a warning sign of incipient overdosage.

Urinary output measurements every 2 hours are important in order to guarantee magnesium excretion in the urine. It is normal for eclamptic patients to have transient oliguria but with magnesium treatment the urinary output should not drop below 25 ml/hour (50 ml per control period of 2 hours).

The respiration frequency is checked every 2 hours and should be at least 12 per minute. When the magnesium dosage is high there is a tendency to poor ventilation due to inadequate function of muscles necessary for thoracic and abdominal respiratory movements.

The magnesium treatment is a preparatory measure before delivery. Once initiated, magnesium treatment should not be interrupted until delivery has occurred. It is advisable to prolong the magnesium treatment until at least 24 hours after delivery.

An alternative treatment is **diazepam**, which should be given IV in doses of 20 mg until convulsions disappear. The disadvantage is that it affects the baby adversely (see page 79).

In case of **recurrent** fits (in spite of treatment with magnesium sulphate or diazepam as above) the 'bolus dose' is repeated IV.

Cerebral malaria

In late pregnancy a woman will run the risk of severe forms of malaria in malaria-affected areas. Cerebral malaria is a feared and dangerous complication, particularly in areas with chloroquine-resistant parasites. Impaired immunity to the parasite during late pregnancy and gradually increasing anaemia pre-dispose to a fatal haemolytic crisis or unconsciousness.

The diagnosis is confirmed by a positive blood film but other forms of diagnosis (meningitis, intoxication, eclampsia) should also be kept in mind.

At delivery, uterine involution will mean a particular risk in cases of severe anaemia very often found in cases of cerebral malaria. The transport of 'anaemic' blood volume from the uterus to the rest of the body may provoke a circulatory collapse leading to pulmonary oedema and death. Blood/volume substitution in cases of high fever, anaemia and unconsciousness should be undertaken with the utmost care. What has been stated regarding eclamptic unconsciousness is also relevant for any other form of unconsciousness. A lateral supine position, indwelling urinary catheter and slight fixation of the patient's hands are advisable measures.

MANAGEMENT   Acute treatment of cerebral malaria can follow a variety of guidelines. The **first** choice should be chloroquine base 300 mg IV or IM followed 8 and 16 hours later by the same dose IM. The total parenteral chloroquine dose is about 900 mg during the first 24 hours.

    The **second** line in cases of cerebral malaria is sulphadoxine (500 mg) + pyrimethamine (25 mg) (Fansidar) and quinine. Sulphadoxine-pyrimethamine is given as a single dose of 3 pills in a gastric tube. In more advanced cases the drug may be combined with quinine. Where there is a threat to life, or if the unconscious woman is in active labour, quinine may be given IV with a dose of 500 mg in 15 ml solution given slowly (at least 10 minutes).

    There are a number of new and alternative drugs for use in chloroquine-resistant cerebral malaria, among which mefloquine is one of the most important. These will not be presented in any detail here.

Meningitis

The unconscious patient with or without convulsions should always be tested for neck stiffness. Lumbar puncture should be performed whenever possible. This is a simple but life-saving diagnostic measure, easily carried out by a skilled nurse/midwife. Early information on the presence of white blood cells in the spinal fluid and early treatment in adequate dosage will save the life of a patient with meningitis. An opalescent spinal fluid is always a sign of purulent meningitis.

MANAGEMENT   The initial treatment of meningitis usually consists of a high dose of benzylpenicillin, 8 g (12 million IU) per 24 hours and chloramphenicol, 1 g every 6 hours, both drugs given intravenously. The possibility of coexisting cerebral malaria or other cause of unconsciousness should always be borne in mind.

Cerebrovascular complications

Sudden unconsciousness, particularly when associated with rapid drop in blood pressure, without signs of eclampsia, cerebral malaria, septic shock, epilepsy or diabetes, may be caused by a vascular complication, cerebral thrombosis, embolism, sub-arachnoid haemorrhage, amniotic fluid embolism etc. There are few diagnostic facilities in poor countries but where available, an ophthalmoscope may be useful for detection of high intra-cranial pressure. A complete neurological examination should be carried out to characterise focal, neurological damage. A lumbar puncture is always advisable but care should be taken not to tap more than a minimum of spinal fluid in case it is bloody. Such patients should be sent to the nearest hospital with resources for intensive care.

Prolapse conditions

Umbilical cord prolapse

This complication will occur in 0.5-1 per cent of deliveries. It may appear without warning but a sudden rupture of membranes and non-engaged presenting part of the fetus is always a dangerous combination. A transverse lie with ruptured membranes is another typical situation, predisposing to prolapse of the cord with acute risk of cord compression. When membranes are bulging and the fetal head or breech is non-engaged, an uncontrolled rupture can easily, particularly in multipara, result in cord complication. In such cases the head should be forced prophylactically into the pelvic inlet by the midwife's outer hand while her inner hand provokes in a controlled way rupture of the membranes once the head is engaged. The entry of a sling of the cord between head and cervical inner wall is thereby avoided ('active rupture of membranes with manually engaged head').

MANAGEMENT   Once detected an umbilical cord prolapse in the cervix, vagina or even outside the vulva should be handled as follows:

The patient should immediately be put in a **knee – chest position** with the level of the pelvis as high as possible (see Figure 26). The woman should always be quickly informed about the serious situation and asked to maintain the uncomfortable knee – chest position.

The examining midwife should immediately try to **insert her whole hand in the vagina** with the intention of **repositioning** the prolapsed cord. Sometimes repositioning is successful but on many occasions the cord sling is impossible to push back above the presenting fetal part. In such cases the midwife's hand is kept in the vagina with two fingers between the presenting fetal part (head or breech) and the inner cervical wall in order to create a space in which the pulsations of the cord can be guaranteed despite the threatening compression. The objective is to achieve good pulsations of the umbilical cord. They may, however, be difficult to palpate and the ultimate criterion of **successful decompression** is the auscultation of fetal heart sounds through the abdominal wall. A normal fetal stethoscope can be used though the position may sometimes make it difficult to hear the fetal heart sounds. A Doppler stethoscope, if available, is an excellent aid in such cases.

Figure 26   A knee – chest position under tocolysis makes the baby 'fall'
            towards the fundus, thereby decompressing a prolapsed cord in
            the cervix.

When cord prolapse occurs in a health unit, the midwife's hand must not
be removed from the vagina as her fingers (in the cervix) guarantee decompression of the cord until the baby is safely delivered by Caesarean section.
This may seem drastic but implies that the midwife has to follow the patient
to the surgical theatre **with her hand inside the patient's vagina** decompressing
the cord and sit beside the patient **during the operation proper.**
A **drug to relax the uterus** (e.g. terbutaline or salbutamol with a dose of 0.5
mg intravenously) is a great help in achieving an immediate tocolytic (uterus-
relaxing) effect, and will greatly facilitate a decompression of the cord in the
knee – chest position as described (see Figure 26).

Prolapse of the cervix or inverted uterus

If the delivering woman suffers from a protracted delivery she may feel a
temptation to bear down too early, before the cervix is fully dilated. A cervical
oedema will often be the result and may even lead to a mechanical obstruction
of delivery. If a vaginal delivery is successfully performed a prolapse of a swollen
and oedematous cervix may occur.

A prolapsed and swollen cervix post partum may be difficult to distinguish
from **uterine inversion**. The latter is usually larger, bleeds more profusely and
the cervical canal is not discernible. It is sometimes the result of forced fundal
pressure from outside together with cord traction for detachment of a retained
placenta.

MANAGEMENT   Cervical prolapse necessitates early bimanual compression of
the prolapsed cervix. The cervix can then fairly easily be forced back through
the vulva. The patient should rest in bed for a couple of days and be treated
with a broad spectrum antibiotic in order to prevent subsequent endometritis.

A uterine inversion must be treated as an emergency. Forced repositioning with the closed fist against the inverted fundus uteri, covered with a saline compress, should be performed without delay. An intravenous dose of 25-50 mg of pethidine will reduce discomfort and pain for the patient. Antibiotics should be given and bed rest is recommended, as with prolapsed cervix.

Retention of the placenta

Expulsion of the placenta occurs normally within 2 hours of expulsion of the newborn. There is no point in forcing the placenta out before this period has elapsed. Expulsion will probably not occur spontaneously after the 2 hours have elapsed.

Management

Retention of the placenta can be managed fairly easily if the correct technique is used. An intravenous dose of 25-50 mg pethidine is given to the mother.

Three hands are needed (Figure 27). The **assistant's hand** should grasp the cord and stretch it carefully. The midwife executing the manual removal of the placenta should put her outer hand on the fundus of the uterus and follow the stretched umbilical cord with her inner hand up to the point where the umbilical cord is attached to the placenta. The amniotic, glossy surface of the placenta is easily recognisable at the site where the umbilical cord joins the placenta.

The **inner hand** then follows the glossy surface to the border of the placenta, trying to identify the placental edge and slowly manipulate the edge in order to achieve a detachment of the placental edge from the uterine wall. It is recommended that the **outer hand** over the fundus of the uterus closely follows the movements and manipulations of the inner hand in order to facilitate identification of the position of the inner hand. In case of doubt (the spatial orientation of the inner hand is sometimes lost) the inner hand should always return to the point where the cord joins the placenta in order to facilitate a reorientation in the uterine cavity. Often the placenta is 'glued' to the uterine wall and it may be quite difficult to detach. Sometimes the placenta must be taken out in pieces but care should be taken not to damage the uterine wall.

Treatment after manual detachment of the placenta should include adequate dosage of a **broad-spectrum oral antibiotic**. In the event of bleeding, oxytocin injections or methylergometrine given orally may be used. Neither of these drugs need be used unless bleeding occurs.

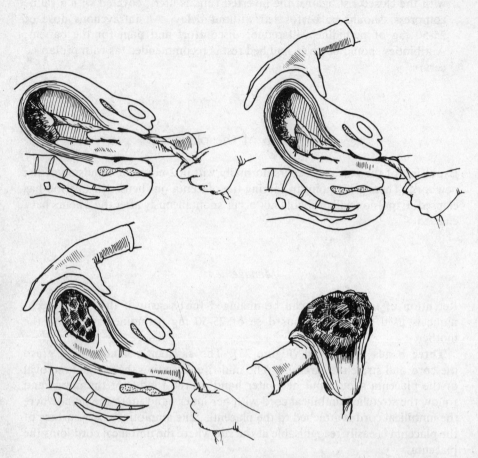

Figure 27   Manual detachment of the placenta requires **three** hands, see text.

Mental disease

The puerperium is associated with an increased incidence of mental disorders, among which the most well-known is the so-called puerperal psychosis. Mental disorders in the puerperium are sometimes difficult to handle even in a hospital. There is an acute risk of the newborn being hurt by a psychotic mother. If possible, lactation should be encouraged to continue but if the psychiatric disorder is serious, the newborn should be taken away from the mother and the mother treated with appropriate drugs, e.g. chloropromazine in a dose of 50 mg IM, which should be repeated until sufficient clinical effect is obtained. It should be underlined that a puerperal psychosis be itself should not be an argument against lactation.

FURTHER READING

1. Chalmers, I., Enkin, M., Keirse, M.J.N.C. *Effective Care in Pregnancy and Childbirth. Volume II: Childbirth.* Oxford University Press: Oxford, 1989.

REFERENCES

1. Pust, R.E., Hirschler, R.A. and Lennox, C.E. Emergency Symphysiotomy for the trapped head in breech delivery: indications, limitations and method. *Tropical Doctor* 1992; **22**: 71-5.

2. Spencer, J.A.D. Symphsiotomy for vaginal breech delivery. Two case reports. *British Journal of Obstetrics and Gynaecology* 1987; **94**: 716-18.

8

Immediate Neonatal Complications
(ASPHYXIA)

Asphyxia at birth

About a million babies die every year as a result of birth asphyxia. Many others will suffer brain damage, often with severe neurological complications due to asphyxia.

It has been estimated that in developing countries, up to 3 per cent of births will result in severe asphyxia requiring resuscitation. Once birth asphyxia is present, it has to be managed urgently at the place of birth.

In developing countries, the majority of births take place at home assisted by a traditional birth attendant (TBA) or a relative. Such assistants do not have the knowledge, skill or technical tools needed for the management of asphyxia. The same is also true, though to a lesser extent, in hospitals where the equipment is frequently out of order.

Consequently, a better awareness of the problem and increased skills in the control of birth asphyxia, have been recognised as the most cost-effective means of improvement in perinatal care. If the treatment is successful, it will considerably reduce both infant mortality, and the number of handicapped infants.

Strategies in the control of birth asphyxia

Certain conditions during pregnancy are associated with an increased risk of birth asphyxia (e.g. pre-term labour, pre-eclampsia) and early signs of asphyxia may occur during labour (intrapartum asphyxia). Four strategies for controlling birth asphyxia can be identified:

1, Referral of high-risk pregnant women for hospital delivery.

2. Early recognition of pre-natal signs of possible asphyxia (meconium stained amniotic fluid, abnormal fetal heart beat pattern, hyperactive contractions).

3. Management of the newborn with asphyxia, in terms of both urgent and skilled resuscitation.

4. Management of post-asphyctic conditions.

Causes of asphyxia in the newborn

1. Intrapartum asphyxia may depress the central nervous functions in the infant. If depression is severe, it may result in a lack of stimulation to the respiratory centre.

2. Infections such as congenital pneumonia secondary to amniotic fluid infections.

3. In pre-term infants lack of spontaneous breathing may be caused by severe immaturity.

4. Aspiration of meconium or thick mucus, or other disorders of the airways, may impair respiration despite normal nervous stimulation.

5. Drugs given to the mother, e.g. pethidine or anaesthetics, may depress the respiratory centre in the infant.

6. Malformations of the central nervous or respiratory systems.

Clinical signs of asphyxia in the new-born baby

The easiest detectable sign in an asphyxiated child is the absence of consistent crying. This can be observed by any birth attendant and the observation should be followed by further assessment. Breathing and cardiac activity should be observed. For many years the Apgar score has been used to systematise observations on the vitality of the new-born infant. There are many difficulties in the use of this method, however. It is complex and was originally aimed for classifying the condition of infants exposed to obstetric analgesia and anaesthesia.

A new system has been suggested[1] using two parameters only and is shown in Table 1.

TABLE 1
A system for classifying asphyxia in the new born

	Score		
	0	1	2
Breathing:	Absent	Gasping	Regular
Heart beat:	Absent	Slow (<100/min)	Fast (>100/min)

Breathing is assessed by looking at the baby or listening to its cry. Measuring the heart beat requires training. The beat may be felt through the chest wall, seen or felt in the umbilical cord or, if a stethoscope is available, by listening. An observer can easily be trained to differentiate between the abnormally slow frequency (60-80 beats per minute) and the normal fast rate of 140-160 beats per minute by comparing the pulse rate with that of his/her own.

The total score is the sum of the score for respiration and the score for the heart beat. Using this assessment the scores correspond to four categories as shown in Table 2.

TABLE 2

The clinical condition and corresponding score

Condition	Score
A vigorous active child	4
A mildly asphyxiated child	2-3
A severely depressed child	1
A stillborn child	0

In **mild asphyxia** the child will make respiratory efforts but will not cry. The heart rate will be around 100 beats per minute and the muscular tone will be relatively good. The child should be treated with cutaneous stimulation, i.e. patting of the soles or rubbing of the back. This stimulation will usually result in crying. If not, procedures for severe asphyxia should be followed.

The **severely asphyxiated child** will make no respiratory movements during the first minutes of life. The heart rate will be low (below 100 beats per minute) and the muscular tone low. Cutaneous stimulation will be of no use and assisted ventilation must therefore be initiated immediately. The insufflation of air into the lungs will usually result in reflex inspiratory movements and the heart rate will increase. The course of events in severe asphyxia is illustrated in Figure 28. Depending on the degree of the prenatal asphyxia, spontaneous breathing will start sooner or later.

Cleaning the airways

As pre-natal asphyxia often precedes post-natal asphyxia meconium-stained amniotic fluid is often present. This may cause airway obstruction. Airway obstruction is most severe following Caesarean sections where no thoracic compression has taken place before birth.

If no suction devices exist, as is usually the case in home deliveries, or if they are out of order, a combination of **back blows** (see Figure 29), **chest thrusts** and **wiping the oropharynx** with a finger wrapped in gauze is used. The fingers

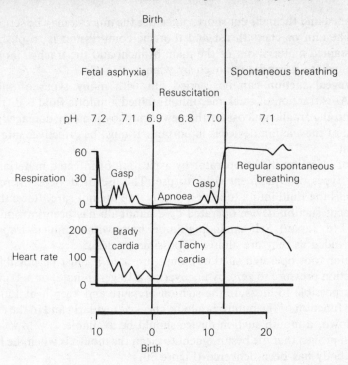

Figure 28 Course of events in severe asphyxia. Before and after birth the heart rate is slower than 100 beats per minute. As soon as resuscitation with effective assisted ventilation has been started the heart rate increases. The spontaneous breathing will occur later and the duration of apnoea reflects the severity of prenatal asphyxia.

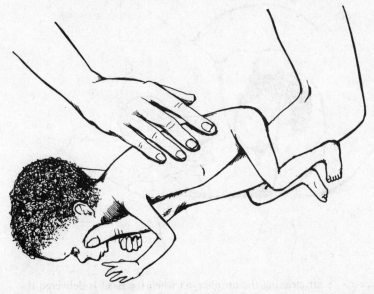

Figure 29 Chest thrust and thoracic compressions can be done without any tools.

must be cleaned and the nails cut short, otherwise the mucosa may be seriously damaged. The aim of chest thrust and thoracic compression is to push the meconium stained material out of the main bronchi and the trachea into the oropharynx, where it can be removed by wiping.

Oropharyngeal suction can be carried out with many types of mucus extractors. As extraction of thick meconium stained amniotic fluid is difficult to handle and the fragile mucosa of the newborn baby is easily damaged, the construction of the suction device is important. It must be effective, safe and easy to clean.

The risk of infection of the operator by aspiration of infected material has made many types of equipment risky to use. The use of devices where the operator sucks the fluid into a tube or a mucus trap are not safe. Recently an effective mucus suction device operated by a handbulb has been introduced. (Blue Cross Ltd, Japan). Self-expanding rubber bulbs without mucus traps are not recommended as they are almost impossible to clean.

If electric or foot operated suction pumps are used it must be possible to drop the suction pressure to zero by uncovering a fingertip hole, or a T-piece. It should be possible to measure the suction pressure and keep it at 150-300 mmHg. The function of the pump should be checked regularly and in the event of a breakdown, a mouth suction device should be available.

It has been proven that the best moment to clean the mouth is when the head but not the body has been delivered (Figure 30).

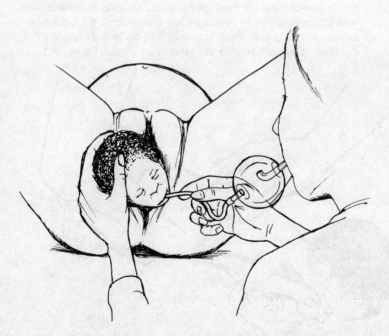

Figure 30   Start cleaning the oropharynx when the head is delivered if meconium stained fluid is present.

Resuscitation scheme

Always clean the oropharynx, and dry and wipe the baby. The resuscitation
scheme is outlined in Table 3.

TABLE 3

Condition of the newborn and actions to be taken

Breathing:	Absent or gasping	Absent	Absent
Heart beats:	Fast	Slow	Absent
Score:	2-3	1	0
Time:			
1 min (at birth)	Cutaneous stimulation until regular breathing starts	Assisted ventilation until regular breathing starts	Assisted ventilation + cardiac massage
2-5 min	Assisted ventilation until regular breathing starts	Change the ventilation procedure: increase volume and pressure, adjust the face mask, clean the airways. Start cardiac massage. If possible intubate and ventilate.	No heart beat: Baby is dead. Discontinue resuscitation.
10-15 min		Give bicarbonate IV + adrenaline.	
30-45 min		Discontinue resuscitation.	

Assisted ventilation

Assisted ventilation should be initiated as soon as possible if spontaneous and
rhythmic breathing is not established with cutaneous stimulation.

In such a case the cord is clamped and cut immediately, and the baby moved
to a resuscitation table. The child should be put in the supine position with the
head lowered and tilted slightly backwards.

In general too much time is spent trying cutaneous stimulation and airway
cleaning. This is a waste of time! Start ventilating the baby and check the effect
by watching for tracheal expansion, feel or listen to the heart rate and monitor
the heart beat by palpation or with the stethoscope (see Figure 31). If possible
two persons should carry out the procedures: one assisting the respiration and
the other monitoring the heart beat.

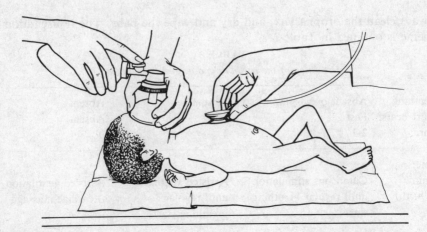

Figure 31   It is important to measure heart rate to assess the effect of
assisted ventilation

Whatever method of ventilation is used, the first breaths require high insufflation pressures (50-70 cmH$_2$O). When the lungs are filled, ventilation is easier
and only 30-40 cmH$_2$O is needed to continue. Ineffective ventilation is caused
either by inadequate insufflation pressure or obstructed airways.

In the event of meconium obstruction the airways may be filled with meconium
and cleaning of the airways may be ineffective.

If no devices for assisted ventilation are available **mouth to mouth ventilation**
should be used (see Figure 32). Air is blown into the nose and the open mouth
using short breaths. Mouth to mouth ventilation, properly practised, is quite
adequate for ventilation of an asphyxiated child for a short period. However,
the risk of cross infection (the midwife or TBA may be infected by the baby
or vice versa) is in many places acknowledged as the main reason for not using
this method.

Figure 32   Mouth-to-mouth ventilation. The air is blown into the baby
through both the nose and the mouth.

The most commonly used artificial ventilation aid is the **bag and mask**. Provided that adequate technique and appropriate equipment are used, 85 per cent of infants with severe asphyxia can be effectively ventilated using this method[2]. No other method or equipment is necessary in such cases.

The bag must:

1. be self-expanding with a volume of approximately 250-300 ml;

2. be easy to take apart for cleaning and sterilisation in boiling water;

3. be easy to put together without risk of malfunctioning and;

4. the rubber of the bag must withstand a tropical climate for at least 2 years.

Many bags have pressure limiting valves. With mask ventilation there is no significant risk of the pressure being too high (due to oesophageal leakage) and valves are not therefore needed. The mask should be easy to fit tight to the face. Soft and circular masks are more effective than the triangular ones.

If the baby has been intubated he may be **ventilated through an endotracheal tube.** There are some disadvantages with this method: the tube might pass into the oesophagus and be ineffective or pass too far down in one bronchus and create a pneumothorax. The method is also difficult to learn. This method should therefore be used only if bag and mask ventilation is ineffective and bradycardia persists. It should be used by someone trained in the procedure.

When intubating, the tube must pass the vocal cords into the larynx and the trachea. The tube can be guided blindly with the index finger of the operator or seen in a laryngoscope. It is important to have the tip of the tube in the correct position and that this is checked after intubation by listening to breathing sounds over both lung fields. If there is no sound over the left lung the tube should be gently withdrawn until sounds can be heard all over the lungs. The procedure is simpler if a tube, marked with black ink over the distal 2 cm in the tracheal end, is used. When the tube is placed in the larynx, the marking should be visible. An alternative is to use an oropharyngeal tube with a tapered tip. With this tube the tip passes between the vocal cords, but the body of the tube is too wide to pass. It is therefore impossible to proceed too far down. When the child starts spontaneous breathing the tube should be removed.

Supplementary oxygen is generally recommended for resuscitation. Oxygen enriched air (50-60 per cent oxygen) should be used. Theoretically use of oxygen enriched air is of uncertain value. The use of 100 per cent oxygen may result in atelectasis (collapse) of the lungs and might well be toxic. In most hospitals, however, pure oxygen is the only gas available.

There are good reasons for assuming that air is as effective as oxygen enriched air in resuscitating babies at birth and there is certainly no reason to refrain from assisted ventilation due to lack of oxygen.

External cardiac massage

External cardiac massage can be attempted if the heartbeat is absent or slow (below 80 beats per minute) and decreasing despite assisted ventilation.

Compress the lower third of the sternum with the operator's thumb pressing the sternum intermittently (100-120 times per minute) and the other fingers supporting the back of the chest. External cardiac massage has a limited effect and should normally not be practised outside hospitals.

Auscultation or palpation of the heart should be performed intermittently. As soon as regular heart beats above 100 beats per minute are recorded the cardiac massage should be stopped. If the heart beats are persistently absent the procedures should be discontinued.

Drugs

INTRAVENOUS BUFFER SOLUTION   If bradycardia persists in spite of adequate assisted ventilation sodium bicarbonate (4 mmol/kg body weight) can be given intravenously through an umbilical vein catheter. The catheterisation should be sterile and the catheter tip should be inserted at least 10 cm behind the umbilicus. The buffer solution should be given slowly over 5 minutes as it is a hyperosmolar solution and can cause cerebral and liver damage.

ADRENALINE   Adrenaline is used to stimulate heart activity when external cardiac massage is given. It can be injected intravenously or given through an endotracheal tube. The dose is 1 ml of a solution 1:10 000. Adrenaline should not be used if severe asphyxia persists for more then 15 minutes after birth.

NALOXONE   Naloxone is a specific antidote to opiates and should be used only if the absence of spontaneous breathing is a result of opiates given to the mother within 5 hours before delivery. Then 0.01 mg/kg is given intramuscularly.

OTHER STIMULATING DRUGS   Lobeline and other stimulating drugs have no place in a resuscitation programme. They are more dangerous than effective.

Duration of resuscitation

It is generally accepted that if 30-45 minutes of continuous efforts at resuscitation with assisted ventilation have not resulted in spontaneous breathing, there is no possibility of a surviving healthy child. It is then recommended that resuscitation be discontinued.

Post-asphyctic treatment

Children requiring resuscitation over a long period before onset of spontaneous breathing (more than 10-15 min) or children presenting with neurological signs of asphyxia (with or without birth asphyxia), irritability, high pitched cry, convulsions or increased/decreased muscular tone must be transferred to a hospital. The most important treatment is phenobarbitone treatment or other anti-convulsive drugs (see page 117).

Training for resuscitation procedures

In order to demonstrate the importance of breathing in relation to time to TBA, health personnel and midwives it is advisable to ask them to hold their own breath and to start a stopwatch. After less than half a minute their discomfort will compel them to breathe.

A home-made manikin with, for instance, a simple ball as a head (15 cm in diameter), can be used for training assisted ventilation. The face mask can be connected to a water manometer for checking the insufflation pressure. High pressure is desirable (50-70 cmH$_2$O) in the first few breaths. Mask and bag ventilation can be taught in this way. Sucking can be taught by asking the TBA to use the suction device and to suck the water out of a glass. Chest thrusts as well as back blows are also best shown on a home-made doll.

Recently a similar training programme was tested among 100 TBAs in the north of India[3] (Figure 33). After training they were all given a bag and mask as well as a suction device and found to be quite skilful. Many of the TBAs later reported that they had succeeded in resuscitating babies which they would normally have looked upon as stillborn in a home delivery.

Transport of pre-term or sick babies

If a baby is sick and there is an option of referring him for treatment, the following questions must be answered:

1. What could be done at the place of delivery, e.g. in terms of warmth and intensified breast feeding?

2. What would be the benefits/risks if the infant is to be sent to a hospital?

Transport should always be avoided until the new-born baby has been rewarmed after birth. This will take 1-2 hours. When the baby is transferred, it should be directly to a hospital where adequate care can be ensured.

The simplest method of transporting the baby is to keep him in direct skin to skin contact with the mother or the accompanying person, e.g. a TBA, a

Figure 33　Assisted ventilation using bag and mask. The procedure can be performed also outside the hospital if the tools are available.

health worker or a relative. In this way, the accompanying person can also feel the muscle tone, the breathing and spontaneous movements of the baby.

It is desirable that a description of the maternal obstetric history and all events during labour and delivery are sent together with the baby to allow the receiving physician to take care of the baby in an appropriate manner.

If a pre-term and/or sick baby has to be transferred to a hospital it is important that the clinical condition of the baby does not deteriorate during transport. Only at well-equipped hospitals will a modern transport incubator be available. If so it has to be warm (35°C) before it leaves the hospital. The batteries of the incubator must be well-charged and the oxygen cylinder, if available, be filled with extra oxygen. A transport incubator may well be locally produced and heated by a large water tank (about 10 litres of warm water placed at the bottom of the box). A mucus extractor and a bag and mask must accompany the baby, and be used if the baby stops breathing or vomits during transport.

FURTHER READING

1.　King, M. *et al: Primary Child Care. A Manual for Health Workers. Book one.* Oxford University Press: Oxford, 1978.

REFERENCES

1. Sterky, G., Tafari, N., Tunell, R. *Breathing and Warmth at Birth*. SAREC Report R2, Stockholm, 1985.

2. Palme-Kilander C. Methods of resuscitation in low Apgar score infants. *Acta Paediatrica* 1992; **81**: 739-44.

3. Raiha, N., Kumar, V. Management of birth asphyxia by traditional birth attendants. *World Health Forum* 1989; **10**: 243-48.

9

The Complicated Puerperium

As has been pointed out earlier in this book, the post-delivery period is a highly vulnerable one for the mother and her new-born baby. A mother who is ill will have problems in breast-feeding and caring for her baby. Also, a large proportion, almost two-thirds, of maternal deaths occur in fact after actual childbirth, and the survival chances of the newborn whose mother has died are small.

Excessive bleeding and anaemia

The **anaemic** parturient woman has a lower tolerance to bleeding during delivery than the non-anaemic: the danger of excessive bleeding will therefore depend on the degree of pre-delivery anaemia. In **pre-eclamptic** parturients **hypovolaemia** is the rule. The reduced blood volume makes such women particularly vulnerable to blood loss.

The immediate, severe post-delivery haemorrhage has been described in the section on delivery complications, and management including aortic compression, drug-enhanced uterine contraction and surgical repair of lacerations was stressed. During the days subsequent to surviving such an episode the woman will be anaemic, and often easily infected. A weak, pale, feverish woman unable to care for or breast-feed her baby is not uncommon.

Management

In the acute episode, **the first priority is to control the haemorrhage by aortic compression** and to substitute fluids, thereby preventing/treating circulatory collapse. One or preferably two heavy gauge intravenous needles enable rapid IV infusion of several 1000 ml of liquids. Putting extra pressure on the infusion by raising the infusion bottle very high, or by compressing the plastic infusion bag, will speed up infusion. The primary objective of treating the bleeding woman intravenously with liquids is to maintain the central arterial blood pressure, avoiding shock (circulatory collapse). Thus the liquids may be saline, sugar solutions or other IV liquids. Lack of red blood cells may, on the other hand, particularly in the severely anaemic woman, manifest itself as dyspnoea (lack of breath). Oxygen treatment may be useful, while waiting for blood transfusion. Blood for transfusion purposes is an important emergency tool in obstetrics, and the organization of transfusion services is discussed on page 148.

The risk of transmitting infections – HIV is most important today – is often considerable, and blood transfusion should, of course, only be performed when absolutely necessary. A blood transfusion can, however, often save life in the immediate post-delivery period.

If the woman has survived the first 4-8 hours after delivery without a blood transfusion, and her circulation is stable, a blood transfusion can usually be avoided. It may in such cases be wiser to treat the anaemia of the puerperal woman, whose circulation is stable but is generally weak, with iron, folic acid, antimalarials and, where appropriate, drugs against hookworm, as well as antibiotics if infection arises. The severely anaemic woman may need a considerable period to recover in the puerperal ward if blood transfusion is to be avoided.

Infections

The post-delivery period makes the woman vulnerable to general infections such as malaria, and to infections entering the body through birth lesions such as lacerations of the vagina or cervix. All interventions also increase the risk of infections: operative delivery, catheterisation of the bladder, or poor hygiene during vaginal examination performed by trained or untrained staff.

The diagnosis may be difficult to establish. A foul-smelling vaginal discharge, long or operative delivery make endometritis – myometritis or other genital infections probable. Urinary tract infection should always be suspected and looked out for, (see below). Respiratory symptoms make pneumonia probable, especially if the woman has been unconscious after, for example, eclampsia or heavy sedation. Engorged breasts often give rise to rapid attacks of fever, but are managed without antibiotics unless a distinct mastitis with the formation of an abscess occurs. Feverish attacks without focal symptoms may indicate malaria, and a blood smear should be taken and examined. Opportunistic infections in an HIV-infected woman may be very varied and difficult to diagnose.

Management

Endometritis – myometritis is treated with oral antibiotics. **There is no reason to give drugs to achieve uterine contraction (methylergometrine or others) in**

cases of endometritis – myometritis, unless there is abundant haemorrhage. Most uncomplicated cases respond dramatically to ordinary penicillin, while infections complicating surgical interventions will demand a broader spectrum of antibiotics. Gonorrhoea and chlamydia may also give rise to puerperal genital infection and must be treated according to local resistance patterns. Malaria treatment will also depend on local resistance factors and the drugs available.

Normally there is no advantage in injecting antibiotics if tablets can be used – all unnecessary injections should be avoided to prevent the risk of HIV transmission.

A good rule is to keep the mother in the health unit until she has maintained a normal temperature for at least 2 days, is only slightly anaemic, is breast-feeding and generally caring for her baby.

Diseases of the urinary tract

Lower urinary tract

Lower urinary tract infection (= infection of the urinary bladder and/or urethra) should be suspected if the woman feels pain when urinating or urinates much more often than usual. Urinary tract infections in general are more common during pregnancy and after delivery. It is wise to examine women with such symptoms, if possible, for gonorrhoea and chlamydia, as well as examining the urine in a microscope after centrifuging it.

MANAGEMENT   Lower urinary tract infections normally respond readily to simple antibiotic treatment. If a woman has repeated infections a predisposing factor can often be found, for instance lesions in the bladder after *Schistosoma hematobium* (bilharzia) infection.

Upper urinary tract

Upper urinary tract infection refers to infection of the renal pelvis or pyelitis. These infections are more serious than bladder infections, as kidney infections may lead to permanent renal damage. Pyelitis normally causes a rise in temperature and local pain. The kidney is often very tender on examination, especially when given a gentle thump from behind.

MANAGEMENT   Upper urinary tract infection should be treated with relatively high doses of a broad spectrum antibiotic.

Trauma

Trauma to the urinary tract may occur either after a very protracted delivery or after delivery using instruments. The sign of bladder trauma is bloody urine (haematuria).

MANAGEMENT   Management consists of bladder drainage through an open catheter until the haematuria clears up. If it is judged that the risk of necrosis in the bladder wall is very high – the woman has been bearing down during many hours of labour and haematuria is gross – then bladder drainage is extra important to prevent the development of a fistula between the bladder and vagina. In such cases the balloon at the tip of the catheter inside the bladder should not be filled but left empty since a filled balloon may contribute to the development of a fistula. The catheter should instead be fixed to the vulva.

Over-extended urinary bladder

If the woman has been in labour for a very long time without being able to urinate – and has not received professional help to empty her bladder during labour – she may have an over-extended bladder after delivery, and be unable to urinate voluntarily.

MANAGEMENT   Management consists of emptying the bladder with a catheter at 4-6 hour intervals for a day or two. If the woman can still not empty her bladder after this time, bladder drainage through a continuous catheter for a few days is recommended. It is important that over-extension of the bladder is avoided; and should this occur, that it is detected and treated early. The woman may otherwise suffer permanent bladder problems, eventually leading to repeated infections etc.

Hypertension

The risk of eclampsia gradually falls during the first 2-3 days after delivery, and after 3 days eclampsia is very rare. It should be remembered that approximately 25 per cent of eclamptic fits occur among puerperal women, often quite unexpectedly.

Management

A woman with severe pre-eclampsia must thus stay in the health unit, under close supervision, for 3-4 days after delivery. By this time, the blood pressure has usually begun to fall. During the first 24-48 hours post-delivery, and especially the first few hours after delivery, the risk of eclamptic convulsions is high in a pre-eclamptic woman. The treatment is as described earlier: sedation, anti-convulsants, and antihypertensive treatment. Often the single most effective and easy to use drug is magnesium sulphate, using the previously described dosage (see page 70).

A particular complication after severe pre-eclampsia or eclampsia is renal insufficiency, at times with anuria. Failure to produce urine means that the woman must be given only around 500 ml of fluid per day. If she is unconscious this can be given as 30 per cent glucose via a gastric tube, to provide calories in the restricted amount of daily fluids. If conscious, it should be given by mouth.

A persistently high blood pressure after delivery should lead to out-patient follow-up with renal function check-up, and investigation for chronic urinary tract infection.

Psychological aspects

After a serious perinatal complication in mother or child, it is important to discuss the problem with the mother and her husband. They must be informed about the possible causes of the complication, and how to prevent a similar complication recurring in following pregnancies. Follow-up of mother and child is advisable, and it is necessary to have a dialogue with both parents about this.

FURTHER READING

1. *The Prevention and Management of Post-partum Haemorrhage.* WHO: Geneva, 1990.

10

Subsequent Neonatal Complications

Respiratory disorders

The early clinical detection of pulmonary disease is essential for clinical management since it makes early treatment possible.

The clinical picture of lung disease in the newborn is fairly similar irrespective of cause. The most important signs are:

1. Tachypnoea, i.e. a respiratory rate above 60 breaths per minute.

2. Increased respiratory efforts with intercostal retractions of the chest.

3. Grunting respiration, caused by the infant holding its breath for a short while at the end of inspiration and then expelling the air with an audible sound.

4. Cyanosis, grey or pale skin colour.

Wet lung disease (transient tachypnoea or pulmonary adaption syndrome)

The cause is profuse production or impaired resorption of the clear fluid which fills the alveolar space during fetal life. This is the most common condition and it usually occurs in pre-term infants or follows asphyxia or Caesarean section. The clinical signs may be quite impressive during the first hours after birth but the condition usually improves gradually and the prognosis is generally good.

Respiratory distress syndrome (RDS, hyaline membrane disease)

This condition is due to insufficient production of surfactant in the alveoli. The result is that the alveoli partly collapse at the end of each breath. Every new breath is in a way almost as difficult as the first. Lack of surfactant has been demonstrated in 20-30 per cent of all infants born before 35 weeks gestation. The clinical signs usually increase gradually during the first days after birth and reach their maximum on the third day. If the child survives, the symptoms will then gradually disappear.

Meconium aspiration

This condition occurs mainly in full-term babies who have suffered intrapartum asphyxia. If meconium is present in the amniotic fluid the material may be aspirated if the child has breathing movements in the womb or while passing through the delivery canal. The aeration of the lungs will be uneven with collapsed areas. The breathing movements are heavy and symptoms appear from the first minute. The skin and the mucous membranes are usually stained by the meconium.

Congenital pneumonia

The infant may have been infected by bacteria from the birth canal of the mother. Clinical signs, as described above, will develop during one of the first days of life and may be associated with poor sucking, apnoeic spells, fever or hypothermia and general hypotonia. Such children need intensive antibiotic treatment and respiratory support.

Management

If the child is **moderately ill** with good spontaneous breathing, oxygen and air under normal pressure can be used. In this situation there is no need to have air under pressure available (compressed air). A concentration of 40-80 per cent oxygen can be achieved by using a **venturi valve**. The oxygen stream sucks air into the valve, thereby creating an oxygen – air mixture which is directed into a facemask or a hood. Venturi valves are available at low cost. A flow of 7-8 litres/min of oxygen is required.

A concentration below 40 per cent oxygen can be achieved with the use of **low-flow oxygen** into a nasal catheter. A flow of 0.1-0.5 litres/min will result in 25-40 per cent oxygen in the inspired air with the mixture of oxygen and air in the airways of the child.

If the child's condition worsens the air – oxygen must be given either under **continuous positive airway pressure (CPAP)** or **intermittent positive pressure ventilation (IPPV)**. Both these methods require that air is available under pressure (compressed air). As the gas is administered directly into the airways it must be humidified and warmed, and the oxygen content monitored. The safest and cheapest method of controlling pressure in the gas stream is to use a water lock.

In CPAP the humidified warm gas – air mixture is pressure controlled by a waterlock, and connected to a nasal catheter by a T-piece with a variable leakage. A CPAP of 2-6 cmH$_2$0 is normally used. In wards with limited resources CPAP is an extremely cost-effective method and when used in a correct way and at an early stage about 80 per cent of infants with respiratory problems will be successfully treated[1].

Should IPPV be necessary and no ventilator is present the pressure of the waterlock can be increased to 20-30 cmH$_2$0, the nosepiece changed to a good facemask, and the end of the T-piece intermittently blocked by the finger. This simple system allows intermittent positive pressure ventilation for hours and can often solve the acute problem.

The use of ventilators is not discussed here. This is part of neonatal intensive care and the reader is referred to standard text books.

Control of oxygen treatment: both too much oxygen, leading to hyperoxia, and too little oxygen, resulting in hypoxia, must be avoided. In immature babies, **hyperoxia** may result in blindness as a result of retrolental fibroplasia. Pure oxygen is also most probably toxic to the lung tissue. **Hypoxia** results in metabolic acidosis, apnoea and hypothermia which might end in death of the child. Oxygen therapy judged according to clinical condition implies that the oxygen content is regulated so that cyanosis just disappears.

In almost all cases **antibiotic therapy** is needed. A combination of penicillin and gentamycin is recommended, combatting the most common bacteria invading the lungs (see page 140).

Good **thermal control** in incubators or from water-filled heated mattresses is a prerequisite for this care. Hypothermia as well as hyperthermia must be avoided (see page 101).

Nutrition given intravenously or by gavage feeding is equally important. The supply of adequate amounts of calories is necessary if the child is to have a chance of coping with the extra work involved in breathing caused by the lung disease.

Low birth-weight babies

The percentage of babies born with a birth weight below 2.5 kg varies considerably from country to country (Figure 34). In fact it is an indicator of the general health situation and living standard in a given country[2]. In many parts of the world low birth-weight babies are the dominating group in death statistics.

With the use of intrauterine growth charts, where birth-weight is plotted against gestational age, it is possible to distinguish low birth-weight infants who have grown appropriately for their gestational age and are born pre-term (normal intrauterine growth) from those who are light or small for gestational age (intrauterine growth retardation), see Figure 35. In the latter group the infants must be subgrouped according to gestational age in the categories 'term' and 'pre-term' infants with growth retardation.

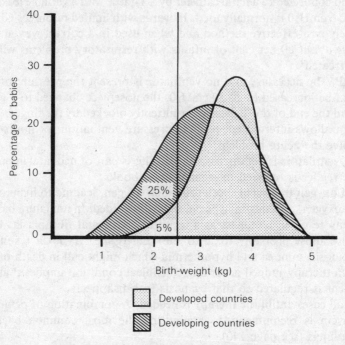

Figure 34 The birth-weight distribution curve reflects the socio-economic situation and to some extent genetic factors. In many developing countries a large proportion of the babies are born with a low birth-weight and these babies contribute to a high perinatal mortality.

Intrauterine growth retardation

These babies are lighter than normal for their gestational age. They consist of different types of babies with different prognoses.

ASYMMETRICAL GROWTH RETARDATION   This occurs when weight is abnormally low compared with length. In many parts of the world where severe maternal malnutrition is prevalent, e.g. in India and parts of Africa these infants constitute up to 30 per cent of the total number of new-born infants. Their birth-weight may be between 2000 and 2500 g and their head circumference and length is in most cases normal for full-term infants i.e. 36 cm head circumference and 50 cm length. They suffer from **prenatal malnutrition**. Other causes are **multiple pregnancy and pre-eclampsia**. In such situations the placental nutritional supply is inadequate. The baby may be born at term or pre-term. The main problems of these infants are:

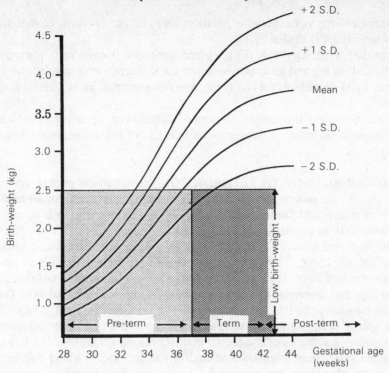

Figure 35 The diagram shows the relation between gestational age and birth-weight. It makes it possible to classify a low birth-weight baby and differ between a term, but small for gestational age, baby from a pre-term baby. The pre-term baby is either appropriate for gestational age (within two standard deviations (S.D.) of the mean) or a growth retarded baby (more than two standard deviations below the mean).

Neonatal hypoglycaemia As they do not have any fat stores at birth but do have a high metabolic rate it is important that starvation does not continue after birth. Food from the fat stores should instead be replaced by appropriate early feeding with breast milk within 1-2 hours after birth. These babies are easy to feed and take large amounts of breast-milk. In cases of hypoglycaemia (blood glucose values below 1.5 mmol/litre) clinical signs such as convulsions, apnoeic spells or other neurological symptoms can occur. Intravenous glucose infusion with 10 per cent glucose 150 ml/kg bodyweight is recommended and if hypoglycaemia persists steroid treatment with hydrocortisone 2.5 mg/kg IV every 12 hours should be started. Both treatments can be withdrawn within a few days when feeding has started and the blood sugar level is stable and normal.

Meconium aspiration and neonatal asphyxia These occur when labour and delivery result in both pre-natal and neonatal asphyxia, with possible aspiration of meconium. This may be the reason for such late neurological complications as intracranial haemorrhage and convulsions, contributing to neurological disability.

Prognosis   With good care the long-term prognosis in cases with late growth retardation is good and, provided pre-natal starvation is not followed by post-natal starvation, the child will grow fast and catch up any initial weight loss.

If, however, the pre-natal period is followed by severe post-natal starvation the situation is dangerous and the risk of permanent brain damage high.

SYMMETRICAL GROWTH RETARDATION   Symmetrical growth retardation covers two groups: the first group consists of **genetically small babies**. Short mothers and fathers often have small children who are born prematurely. Often social factors and an early teenage pregnancy are feature in the maternal history. These babies usually have small heads and normal skin-fold thickness. They will remain small and their prognosis is good.

Other babies have very early intrauterine growth retardation either due to **embryopathy, maternal diseases, infections, drug or alcohol abuse**. These babies may have small heads, short stature and low birth-weight. They often have special clinical findings such as low set ears, a broad nose and general hypotonia. In some cases congenital malformations are present and in some so-called syndromes stigmata and malformations occur. These babies are frequently also brain damaged with poor growth and development though in many cases the true reason for the early growth retardation cannot be determined.

Thus pre-term growth retarded babies constitute a varied group and the **outcome** can vary between severe persistent growth retardation and psychomotor retardation, to completely normal growth and development. In many cases it is not possible to make a distinct diagnosis at birth, or ascertain to which group the child belongs until it has reached 6 months of age or more.

Pre-term babies

In most developing countries the efforts of saving pre-term babies start when the babies have reached 28 weeks of gestation or a birth-weight of more than 1000 g. In developing countries this is a necessity due to limited economical and personal resources. The costs of modern neonatal intensive care for infants born between 24 and 28 weeks of gestation are enormous. Such costs are almost impossible to cover in the industrialised world and would more or less consume all resources for health services in a developing country.

For infants born at 28-37 weeks of gestational age the main problems are discussed below. The various disorders are discussed in other parts of the book and we refer to the relevant sections: asphyxia at birth (page 78); RDS (page 95); hyperbilirubinaemia (page 112); hypothermia (page 101) and nutritional problems (page 107).

ASSESSMENT OF MATURATION OF LOW BIRTH-WEIGHT BABIES   Due
to the difference in the pattern of diseases and outcome it is of considerable
clinical interest to find out if a low birth-weight baby is born pre-term or
at term. If the maternal menstrual data is accurate there is no problem in
calculation. If the data is absent or inaccurate it is of some help to use a
maturation scoring system. Ideally such a system should be based on maturation data from the same country as there are considerable genetic differences
in maturation between different ethnic groups.

There is no current scoring system that has been tested in a number of
developed and developing countries.

In the opinion of the authors, a scoring system based on external and easily
defined signs is preferable to systems including neurological signs, as these
are influenced by the time after birth and by the general condition of the
baby. An example of such a comparatively simple scoring system[3] is presented
in the table below. This method has been widely used in Sweden and has also
been found reliable when validated against other methods (Table 4).

There is a tendency for all maturation scoring systems to underestimate
the gestational age of children with intrauterine growth retardation. There
is also a considerable margin of error in the determination of gestational age
when using a scoring system. No system gives a more accurate estimate of
gestational age than ± 2 weeks.

From the clinical point of view the most important maturation function
is the capacity to suck milk from the mother's breast. A pre-term baby born
before 33-35 weeks of gestation can not usually suck and thus requires special
assistance (see page 110).

Hypothermia and neonatal cold injury

During the past two decades hypothermia has been recognised as a problem
in tropical countries. This has previously not been thought to be the case since
room temperature in these countries is usually high, at least in the daytime.
Also, body temperature has usually been measured with rectal thermometers
which do not record temperatures below 35°C. Thus the temperature of a baby
admitted to a neonatal ward has been reported to be 35°C though the actual
temperature might actually have been as low as 30°C.

Recent systematic investigations of body temperature of babies in several
developing countries have shown that 2-12 hours after birth about 80 per cent
of the babies have a rectal temperature of less then 36°C and that a body
temperature between 32 and 34°C is particularly common in babies with low
birth-weight.

Already at the beginning of this century it was shown by Budin that pre-term
babies with a rectal temperature of less than 36°C had a mortality rate of 80
per cent. If they were kept at a rectal temperature above 36°C, the mortality
rate dropped to only 20 per cent.

TABLE 4
Finnström maturation score

	Score			
	1	2	3	4
Breast tissue	5 mm	5-10 mm	10 mm	
Breast nipples	Hardly visible	Well defined	Edge of areola lifted	
Skin vessels	Big vessels visible over abdomen	Some veins and branches visible	A few vessels visible	No vessels visible
Hair quality	Thin and woolly	Thick silk-like hair		
Finger nails	Do not reach the finger-tip	Reaching finger-tip but distal and not distinct	Reaches or passes finger-tip. Distal and distinct. Nails hard	
Ear cartilago	No cartilago in antitragus	Cartilago in antitragus	Cartilago in antihelix	Starts to be cartilago in the whole ear also in helix
Skin lines in sole of foot	No lines visible	No lines in the back ⅔ of the foot	Some lines over the fore ⅔ of the foot	The whole sole has lines

Points	Gestational age (weeks)
7	27
8	28
9	29
10	30
11	31
12	32
13	33
14	33
15	34
16	35
17	36
18	37
19	38
20	39
21	40
22	41
23	42

Helix
Antihelix
Antitragus
Tragus

In Sweden there is great experience with the Finnström maturation score. This score
has been tested against other scores and found to be most reliable
From: *Acta Paediatrica Scandinavica* 1977; **66**: 601-4.

Keeping babies warm is probably the most important single factor in reducing neonatal mortality among pre-term and low birth-weight babies. It has been estimated that during the last decades, prevention of hypothermia has contributed to a 25 per cent increase in survival rate in industrialised countries.[4]

TABLE 5

The relationship between degree of hypothermia and neonatal mortality

Birth weight (g)	Body temperature (°C)			
	< 32.0	32.0-33.9	34.0-35.9	> 36.0
Under 1500				
Deaths (% mortality)	91 (70.0)	79 (54.4)	70 (48.2)	10 (30.3)
Cases	130	145	145	33
1500-2499				
Deaths (% mortality)	96 (51.1)	100 (28.7)	135 (22.5)	53 (18.9)
Cases	188	349	599	280
Over 2499				
Deaths (% mortality)	31 (52.5)	55 (41.0)	107 (19.9)	107 (13.2)
Cases	59	134	538	811
Standardised mortality risk ratio	7.28	4.58	1.63	1.00

From: Tafari, N. Hypothermia in the tropics: epidemiological aspects. In: Sterky, G., *et al. Breathing and Warmth at Birth*. SAREC Report No. 2, Stockholm, 1985).

Main causes of hypothermia

Underweight babies have **decreased heat insulation** due to lack of subcutaneous fat. This results in a raised skin temperature and a subsequent increase in heat loss.

They also have an **extensive surface area in relation to body weight**. The surface area is two to three times larger in new-born babies than in adults in relation to body weight. This increases all types of heat loss: radiant, convective, conductive and evaporative. Thus, for an underweight new-born baby at an environmental temperature of 23°C the heat loss is approximately equivalent to an environmental temperature of 0°C for an adult and results in rapid cooling of the baby. For a naked baby a comfortable environmental temperature is 35-37°C and for a cot nursed term baby the room temperature should be more than 25°C.

During the first few days after birth the **metabolic response to exposure to cold is limited** and the risk for hypothermia is thereby increased.

When feeding is started and the baby starts to increase in weight the metabolic response to cold improves, resulting in better thermal stability.

In **hypoxia**, metabolic response to cooling is absent, easily leading to hypothermia after asphyxia and pulmonary disorders.

If the baby is **starving after birth** there will not be any increase in its metabolic rate when exposed to cold. The baby will then become hypotonic and lack sucking reflexes. A vicious cycle will thus start, ending in a malnourished, severely hypothermic baby (see Figure 36).

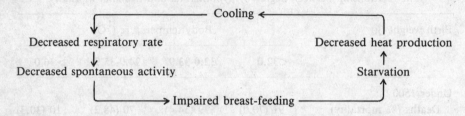

Figure 36   The interaction between lack of breast-feeding and development of hypothermia.

A cold, starved baby becomes easily infected as demonstrated by the well-known situation of a 2 kg baby with sclerema, pulmonary bleeding, who ultimately dies on admission at 2 weeks of age. This is, in fact, a situation that can be prevented.

Clinical signs of mild and severe hypothermia

Mild hypothermia has been defined as a rectal temperature between 28 and 34°C. Severe hypothermia is present when the body temperature is below 28°C.

The typical clinical picture in mild as well as in severe hypothermia may include some or all of the following signs:

- Lethargy and hypotonia
- Slow heart rate and slow respiratory rate
- Weak crying
- Absence of movements
- Peripheral oedema and sclerema (hard oedema on the legs and the back)
- Erythema of the face giving the impression of a healthy child
- Pulmonary bleeding with blood-tinged secretion in the mouth and severe intercostal retractions
- Cold skin over the whole body and not just the peripheral parts.

The clinical diagnosis is confirmed by measuring the body temperature with a thermometer that registers at least as low as 25°C. Such thermometers are available from UNICEF, but are seldom used. Every institution caring for new-born babies ought to have at least one such thermometer. Axillary temperature has been shown to give the same result as rectal temperature provided the thermometer is placed high up in the axilla.

Prevention of hypothermia

Severe hypothermia is due more to lack of knowledge than to lack of equipment. The main points in a strategy to combat the problem are:

1. Avoid evaporative heat loss at birth by **drying** the baby.

2. Use the **skin-to-skin** contact with the mother as a safe and effective method of providing extra heat.[5]

3. **Special care** is needed for **underweight and pre-term babies** and other high risk babies.

It is important to **avoid heat loss through evaporation**, so within the first minute after birth a newborn baby should be dried, wrapped and given to the mother (Chapter 4). A naked baby loses more heat than it can produce and will thus rapidly become hypothermic. Wrapping the baby is effective in preventing heat loss provided the wrapping material is dry. The degree of insulation depends on the amount of air enclosed in the wrapping. The more layers of clothing the more effective the wrapping. The head should also be covered.

The safest and most effective way of providing the baby with extra heat is **direct skin-to-skin contact with the mother** as soon as possible after birth. This should be practised whenever possible.

Pre-term and underweight babies must be cared for with special attention:

1. The temperature of the room must be kept as high as possible and at least at 30-32°C.

2. The baby should be wrapped in extra blankets.

3. All necessary undressing (i.e. to weigh or clean) should be performed as quickly as possible.

4. Skin temperature should be checked repeatedly by touching the baby. Cool feet and hands indicate cold stress.

5. Avoid heating by hot water bottles, hot stones or uncontrolled radiant heaters. Use skin to skin contact with the mother using the 'kangaroo method' if extra heat is necessary and air heated incubators or other controlled heat sources are not available.

Treatment in hospitals

It is generally agreed that mild hypothermia is best treated by fast rewarming, provided that the method is safe and does not result in local burns. Burns might easily occur when using focused radiant heat sources or uncontrolled methods such as hot water bottles or heated stones. These methods should be replaced by the safe and effective method of using skin to skin contact which can never cause burns and which has been shown to be effective in rewarming mildly hypothermic babies.

Where severe hypothermia is concerned, there has been a great deal of controversy regarding the speed of rewarming. The results of recent studies in adults as well as in the newborn have shown that fast rewarming gives a better survival rate than slow rewarming. An intravenous infusion with 10 per cent glucose during rewarming is recommended in order to avoid hypoglycaemia.

There is also controversy over the method of providing heat for the infant. One alternative is to **keep the room temperature high.** The advantage with this method is that it is inexpensive. The disadvantages are firstly, however, that both mother and staff find a temperature of 30-32°C unbearable for long periods and secondly that all infants in the room are treated with the same environmental temperature. If no other controlled heat source is available this method is the best choice and the room can then be heated by any locally available method such as a fire or a stove. In the tropics the use of solar energy for warming water, which can then be transferred to a heating element in a room, is an effective method and will in the future probably be of great importance.

The mother can be used as a source of extra heat – the 'kangaroo method'. There are many obvious advantages with this. One is the closeness to the mother's breast for breast feeding, another is the attention provided, which the baby needs even at referral centres.

Heating a bed using the heat from electrical bulbs below the bed and covering the bed with a Plexiglass cover is a method practised in many hospitals. This ensures an environmental temperature of 35°C provided the number of heating bulbs is regulated regularly according to the temperature of the bed. This method has the advantage of being simple and can be maintained by equipment available locally. The effectiveness of this method may be improved by replacing the ordinary mattress with a bag filled with water. If the water is kept at 37°C it is an effective alternative to the incubator.

The water-filled heated mattress is a new device that has been tested in different industrialised as well as developing countries. The mattress is filled with 10 litres of water heated by an electric heater. The temperature of the water can be regulated at between 35-38°C. One of the advantages with this method is that the water will remain warm for up to 2 to 3 hours even when disconnected from the electricity supply[6].

The mattress is used in an ordinary cot and the infants are dressed and covered by a blanket. The method is an alternative to the expensive and complex air heated incubators and the 'kangaroo method'.

It is also possible to keep babies warm by **radiant heat.** However there is increasing concern about this method in continuous care. Exposure to the environment including air and the hands of staff, increased evaporative heat loss and difficulties in providing sufficient warmth as well as concern about possible eye damage caused by the infra-red light has led to this equipment being used mainly as a tool in emergency situations, rather than as a method for long-term treatment.

Heating lamps and parabolic infra-red heaters are dangerous. Lamps may explode and burn the baby, and overheating by parabolic collimators can easily occur.

Air-heated incubators are effective and the most used device in industrialised countries. There are advantages with this method. The child has surroundings separated from the outside environment which gives him some protection against infections if the child is alone and the incubator is clean. It is also possible to inspect the child naked and look for spontaneous movements, colour and respiration. There are, however, considerable disadvantages. The contact with the mother is disrupted, and there is an increased risk of infections if the incubator is not cleaned properly or if more than one child is in the incubator. There is always the risk of dysfunction of the incubator. Experience has shown that a 'sense of magic' will easily develop, making the staff rely too much on the machine and forget to check the condition of the infant. In fact in the third world solutions other than incubators should be used to keep infants warm and incubators should only be used for the few infants needing intensive care.

Whatever method is used to keep babies warm, it is of the utmost importance that **the baby and the mother are kept together** and that breast-feeding is started and maintained during the stay in hospital. In developing countries this part of the treatment has the highest priority.

Nourishing the sick baby

Breast-feeding

In most parts of the world, mothers and their new-born babies are discharged after a hospital delivery within the first day of birth. A heavy work load, infections and malnutrition in the mother all contribute to impaired breast-feeding and early malnutrition of the new-born infant. For discussion on breast-feeding, see Chapter 5.

The importance of exclusive breast-feeding has been illustrated in recent studies from developing countries[7]. The incidence of gastrointestinal infections has been found to be much higher in infants who have been given water or other supplements to the breast-milk. The reason could possibly be contamination of the liquids or interaction with the immune defence mechanisms.

In home deliveries there is by tradition often close contact between mother and child and early breast-feeding is initiated. Colostrum is often falsely considered to be harmful and not given to the baby, but thrown away, however. Before introduction of western medicine in the 1940s and 1950s breast-feeding 10-20 times a day was the norm in most cultures. In western medicine a number of recommendations regarding the minimum interval between feeds etc, were introduced. These were not based on valid scientific data and disturbed the natural collaboration between mother and child.

Thus the reintroduction of early contact between mother and child after birth will be the first step on the road to successful breast feeding. During the ensuing days, the following simple rules should be followed:

● Avoid unnecessary separation of mother and child.

● Stimulate frequent sucking.

● Assist the mother in the positioning of the infant so that the infant has a comfortable resting position at the mother's breast and starts sucking with both nipple and areola in its mouth.

● Avoid unnecessary weight checks before and after feeding and restrict weight checks in hospital wards to one a day.

● Do not give any extra fluids or nutrients during the first few months of life to healthy term babies who are gaining weight.

Some properties of human breast-milk

The **antibacterial** aspects of human breast-milk are one of the most important advantages of breast-feeding in the third world. These antibacterial properties consist of immune globulins produced by the mother and are partly active against the mother's own bacteria that will hopefully colonise the baby. Other factors are high levels of lysozyme which counteract the bacterium *Escherichia coli*. Human milk also contains large numbers of macrophages, leucocytes and lymphocytes. It has been calculated that a breast-fed infant ingests each day as many leucocytes as circulate inside the baby.

The result of these and other antibacterial properties of the mother's breast milk is that breast-fed infants have fewer gastrointestinal infections. This includes both pre-term and underweight babies and has been repeatedly shown in many developing countries.

The **nutritional contents** of human milk are extremely well-adapted to the needs of the infant. The calorific content and the balance between different nutrients such as protein, fat and minerals correspond exactly to the demands of the child. Still more important is the fact that most nutrients are more easily utilised by the baby than artificial milk nutrients. Colostrum and pre-term breast milk have a particularly high concentration of valuable calories, proteins and sodium.

Support and **instruction** for the mothers are important tasks for those assisting her on the days after delivery. In most cases, breast-feeding will start with little intervention from other people, though the primipara in particular may need support.

Explain the special properties of breast-milk to the mothers. Particularly the antibacterial effects; and the special characteristics of pre-term breast milk should be emphasised. Explain that colostrum is important and not dangerous for the child.

Try to explain the use of **expressed breast milk** in the case of a sick child or a child too pre-term to be able to suck. Manual expression is a simple and effective method which, for hygienic and economical reasons, is preferable to pumps. The breasts are wiped with a few drops of expressed milk. Milk is then expressed directly into a clean cup or feeding bottle.

Support the mother in periods of breast-feeding problems:

● Sore nipples may need temporary manual expression of milk and attention to the feeding technique.

● Inadequate supply of milk is the likely cause of infants failing to increase properly in weight and the stools turning dark green (so called starvation stools). In this situation more frequent sucking and support of the mother may help. The mother may need to be assisted in her daily work at home in order to find time to rest.

● Adequate intake of food and fluids is also important.

Breast engorgement may occur during breast-feeding. The recommended treatment is to try to start feeding by manual expression of milk and frequent short sucking periods.

INFECTIONS AND TREATMENT OF THE MOTHER WITH DRUGS   Most maternal puerperal infections do not constitute contraindications to breast-feeding. The child has already been infected by the micro-organism and antibiotic drugs are transferred to the child via the breast milk. Breast-feeding is also continued in case of maternal tuberculosis, hepatitis, HIV-infection, malaria etc. (see Chapter 11). Any decision to stop breast-feeding must take into consideration the risk of malnutrition and infection.

Breast-feeding can usually continue even when the mother is taking drugs. There are, however, a few exceptions to this rule such as tetracyclines, sulphonamides and cytotoxic substances. If the treatment is of short duration the mother's milk should be expressed and discarded and when treatment is discontinued breast-feeding can resume.

Alternatives to mother's milk

If a substitute for the mother's breast milk is required **raw milk from wet nurses** is one alternative where this old method is still in use. The wet nurse might be a friend or relative. This may be a better alternative for pre-term babies than diluted cows' milk.

Donated milk: the milk might be expressed breast milk from a mother who has too much breast milk. It might also be 'drip milk', i.e. milk collected during breast-feeding from the breast not sucked by the baby. If the milk is to be used instantaneously it can be used raw if precautions against HIV infection have been taken. Otherwise Holder pasteurisation at 62°C for 30 min is recommended. This will make the milk sterile and also effectively destroy the HIV virus. However, most of the immunological properties of the breast milk are also destroyed by this procedure.

If no human milk is available **cows' milk** must be used. In which case, it must be diluted with two parts milk, one part boiled water and one teaspoon of sugar per 100 ml of diluted milk should be added.

Buffalo milk has a very high fat content. If the cream is removed the composition is similar to cows' milk and can be diluted as cows' milk.

A number of modern modified **cows' milk-based formulae** both for term and pre-term babies are available on the market. Their composition has been modified so that, from a nutritional point of view, they resemble human breast milk. From the nutritional point of view, artificial feeding has no detrimental effects in industrialised countries. In developing countries, however, evidence that breast feeding has a major influence on infant morbidity and mortality is strong and introduction of bottle feeding must therefore be limited to those cases where all other methods have been tried and failed. In this situation the alternative is to give properly prepared and properly administered cows' milk formula.

Alternative feeding methods

Bottle feeding is the most common method for giving milk or formula. The problem with milk bottles is hygiene. Boiling in clean water after proper manual washing is the most effective way of cleaning a bottle. The importance of keeping the bottle clean must be emphasised to the mother. Since there are obvious and well-documented risks with bottle feeding in developing countries, this method should only be used if all other efforts to give the mother's milk have been unsuccessful.

If the child is too small or too ill to suck, **feeding with a spoon** or directly from a cup is the best method. This procedure can be used at home after discharge from the hospital. The method is safe, cheap and has hygienic advantages. Most infants are able to swallow even if they are not able to suck. Spoon and cup feeding is very time-consuming and it is often difficult to know the exact amount the baby gets.

Compressed cotton filled with milk is a method practised in many homes in developing countries. Expressed breast milk is kept in a cup. A piece of cotton is put into the milk cup and then gently compressed in the mouth of the baby. This is an alternative to be remembered when other tools have proved unsuccessful in feeding small preterm babies at home.

Gavage feeding is a method often used in hospitals. It is fast and safe if certain precautions are considered before starting feeding. A thin nasogastric tube should be used. The distance from the mouth to the ear and to the stomach is estimated and marked on the tube.

The tube is installed gently through the nose into the stomach. The position of the tube should be checked by aspiration of gastric content and by injecting a few millilitres of air into the stomach while listening with a stethoscope placed over the stomach. The tube may remain in place for 1-2 days and the feeding takes place intermittently over 15-20 min.

TABLE 6

The amounts of breast milk or formula for different birth weights

	Consumption ml/kg per day						
	Day 1	Day 2	Day 3	Day 4	Day 5	Day 10	Day 14
Birth weight (g)							
800-1200	50	60	70	80	100	150	180
1200-2000	50	60	80	100	120	150	180

Supplementation of breast-feeding in pre-term babies

Iron should be given from 4-8 weeks of age in order to prevent iron deficiency. Two mg/kg per day of iron sulphate is recommended. Also a combination of vitamin D 400 units per day and vitamin A 1000 units per day should if possible be given from 1-2 weeks of age.

Parenteral nutrition

The use of intravenous nutrition should be restricted only to babies in which total peroral (by mouth) feeding has proved impossible. Parenteral nutrition is a supplement to peroral nutrition in most cases. Total parenteral nutrition is used mainly in babies requiring surgery and babies with a birth weight below 1000 g.

The high **risk of symptomatic bacteraemia** (15 per cent or more) is the main reason for restricting parental nutrition in neonatal care. Careful aseptic technique in inserting the cannula into the vein, the use of closed infusion systems and change of infusion solution every 24 hours will reduce the infection rate.

In most infants the intravenous fluid used during the first day is **10 per cent glucose** without any additives. A volume of 50 ml/kg per day is often recommended.

Sodium requirements vary substantially and in the first days requirements are normally low but subsequently increase to 3-4 mmol/kg per day. The **potassium** requirement is about half that of sodium. Electrolyte solutions with high levels of sodium are added to the 10 per cent glucose solution where available.

Glucose and electrolytes are the only intravenous solutions available in most countries in the third world. The need for calories, protein and fat is not covered by these substances. Amino acids and fat solutions are needed to give 'total parenteral nutrition'. These substances are expensive. If they are available they are accompanied by recommendations for use and their use is accordingly not included here.

The **total volume** of intravenous fluids given should be equivalent to the recommended total volume of breast-milk shown in the Table 6.

Preparation of intravenous fluids is usually performed by the ward staff using various solutions in stock. Aseptic conditions must be maintained and accurate monitoring of the amounts administered as well as determination of serum levels of glucose, urea, creatinine, sodium, potassium, albumin and acid – base balance must be carried out to avoid the metabolic complications of parenteral nutrition.

Jaundice in the neonatal period

In some countries the incidence of jaundice is relatively high, for instance, in Japan, parts of Africa and India and in the Mediterranean region. These differences are partly due to genetic differences and may also be due, at least in part, to differences in handling and the supply of nutrients to new-born babies. In most neonatal wards throughout the world jaundice is one of the main problems requiring neonatal care.

Clinical judgment

In the assessment of jaundice some simple criteria indicating a need for neonatal treatment may be helpful:

1. Jaundice within 24 hours after birth is always abnormal.

2. Jaundice in a sick child with, for example, difficulties in sucking or breathing or with abnormal movements is abnormal.

3. Jaundice in pre-term infants is abnormal.

4. Jaundice lasting more than 1 week in a full-term infant or more than 2 weeks in a pre-term infant is abnormal

5. Jaundice in infants with dark urine needs special diagnostic attention as a liver disorder is probable.

Thus jaundice that appears on days 2-7 is a less serious problem in a full-term, apparently healthy infant and might well be handled at a peripheral hospital without a special neonatal unit.

Assessing the degree of jaundice

Clinically it is easy to recognise jaundice when the bilirubin level is 100 μmol/l or more. The degree of hyperbilirubinaemia is, however, very difficult to judge. In black infants the best site for examination is the inside of the lip. The degree of anaemia, polycythaemia and maturation of the skin influences assessment in all neonates. The quality of the light is, thus, of great importance. It is recommended that the examination is made in daylight whenever possible.

In order to improve the clinical judgment the colour of the skin can be compared with the colour of different yellow strips on a Plexiglass pin, the 'icterometer'. With proper training the method could be used as a screening procedure.

There is no good substitute at present for a blood sample and determination of total bilirubin by a spectrophotometric bilirubinometer.

Jaundice in infants with special problems

Pre-term babies have an increased incidence of jaundice. In full-term white infants 5 per cent have bilirubin levels above 200 μmol/l and 1-2 per cent have levels above 250 μmol/l. In pre-term babies the incidence of peak bilirubin levels above 200 μmol/l is about 30 per cent; and above 250 μmol/l, about 15 per cent. The reason for the high incidence of jaundice in pre-term babies is their immature liver enzyme function.

Jaundice is not only more prevalent in pre-term babies but is also more dangerous since the blood – brain barrier is less effective and the albumin binding capacity lower.

Jaundice within 24 hours after birth is dangerous since the bilirubin level in such cases may reach toxic levels within 1 or 2 days. The condition is almost always associated with a blood group incompatibility between mother and child, either in the ABO system (a mother with blood group O and the child with blood group A or B), or within the Rh system; (a Rh negative mother and a Rh positive child). A serological investigation of mother and child, including a Coombs' test, is of great importance. An early blood-exchange transfusion might be necessary. The purpose is to decrease the amount of antibodies circulating, to decrease the level of bilirubin and to treat anaemia (see Appendix V).

In a sick child with, for example, sucking difficulties, abnormal movements, high-pitched crying or breathing difficulties, the possibility that the jaundice may be a complication of perinatal asphyxia, bacterial infection or hypoglycaemia must be kept in mind. Examination of blood culture, chest X-ray and blood sugar are important diagnostic procedures for correct treatment.

Deficiency in glucose-6-phosphate-dehydrogenase is prevalent in East Asia and Africa. A deficiency of this enzyme may trigger off a haemolytic process should the child be exposed to certain special drugs or food. The most important drugs in this respect are antibiotics such as sulphonamides, chloramphenicol, sodium paraminosalicylate (PAS) and nitrofurantoin, antimalaria drugs, antipyretic and analgesic drugs. Even broad beans may trigger off the process. In some areas where this deficiency is prevalent a neonatal screening programme for the disease is used, e.g. in Malaysia.

Breast-milk induced jaundice is the most common reason for prolonged jaundice with no clinical signs (i.e normal size of the liver, normal colour of the urine, good sucking and nutrition and absence of anaemia). The reason for this disorder is still not quite understood but the disease is uneventful and no reports of brain damage due to the disorder are known. Thus there is no reason to interrupt breast-feeding, particularly in the third world. Within a few weeks the jaundice will start to decrease and usually disappears after 4-16 weeks.

Congenital hypothyroidism may be the cause of prolonged jaundice. In such cases the level of serum thyroid stimulating hormone (TSH) should be determined if possible. Other symptoms are constipation, umbilical hernia and thick skin.

Cholestatic jaundice. If the urine is dark and the direct fraction of conjugated bilirubin is increased, bile obstruction is present and further investigations are needed.

Treatment

Phototherapy has been extensively investigated and used during the last 20 years. It has been established that the method is effective and if properly used has no long-term adverse effects on infants. It is thus a method that is regarded as appropriate.

Phototherapy works in such a way that the light converts bilirubin in the skin into an isomer that can be excreted through the liver. The efficiency depends upon the intensity of the light. The usual recommendation is 6-8 light tubes at a distance of 40 cm from the infant. The lamps must be changed every year in order to maintain a constant, high-level light intensity. An effective phototherapy lamp could be produced locally. Special blue lamps that cannot be replaced should be avoided.

To protect the infant from light and from glass splinters in case a lamp might break the tubes must be separated from the infant by Plexiglass, which must be clean.

All babies undergoing phototherapy must have their eyes covered by a piece of dark cloth. During treatment the whole child should be exposed to light and his position varied at fixed intervals.

If the jaundice has reached toxic levels the clinical picture of 'kernicterus' occurs. This is characterised by tonic convulsions, abnormal eye movements and loss of hearing. The mortality is about 50 per cent and almost all survivors develop severe neurological sequelae. There is no effective treatment once this stage of jaundice has been reached. The condition can and should be prevented earlier.

As there is no direct connection between the level of bilirubin in the blood and the risk of brain damage the recommended bilirubin levels are arbitrary and not scientifically proven. A widely used recommendation is to start treatment when the bilirubin level expressed in μmol/l exceeds 1/10 of the weight in grams. A baby weighing 2100 grams should then receive phototherapy when the bilirubin level exceeds 210 μmol/l.

It has been shown that the most effective period of therapy is the first 3 hours. After that the bilirubin in the skin must be restored before therapy is continued. From a practical point of view 1-3 hours' break may be of value to let the child eat.

Blood-exchange transfusion should mainly be used in early and severe jaundice caused either by blood-group incompatibility between mother and child or by septicaemia. The procedure is dangerous and involves a considerable risk of post-operative septicaemia and, during the actual procedure, risk of bradycardia and circulatory failure. A detailed description of the procedure is given in Appendix V.

Neurological disorders

Neurological disorders are a major cause of neonatal morbidity, particularly in developing countries. The dysfunction of the central nervous system is not usually caused by one single factor, but by the interaction of, for example, asphyxia, jaundice, perinatal malnutrition, infection, hypoglycaemia and hypothermia.

Precautions to avoid asphyxia and hypothermia, early feeding and adequate management of hyperbilirubinaemia are some examples of procedures that may diminish the risk of brain damage.

Symptoms of neurological disorders

External signs of **malformations** such as chromosomal aberration, e.g. Down's syndrome may suggest that the infant could be more vulnerable than a healthy child.

An abnormally small or large head is verified by plotting the maximum head circumference of the child in relation to the gestational age. Values below 95 per cent of the normal indicate microcephalus and values above 95 per cent suggest hydrocephalus.

Microcephalus is often due to developmental defects of the nervous system. It will result in an impaired development of the central nervous system and psychomotor retardation. The clinical signs may be apparent at birth, but sometimes it is not possible to diagnose microcephalus until 2-4 months after birth.

An unusually large head may either be normal, due to genetic causes, or abnormal, due to increased intracranial pressure with the presence of hydrocephalus. It is usually possible to palpate the widened sutures of the skull. Increasing intracranial pressure may give the 'setting sun' sign; vomiting and increased fontanelle tension. In such cases a ventricular shunt operation should, if possible, be performed urgently.

Impaired hearing: may be caused by jaundice, congenital abnormalities such as external ear malformations or viral infections during pregnancy. It is usually possible to establish whether or not the baby reacts to the voice of the mother or the examiner, by testing for instance if it turns its head towards the sound.

Inability to suck could be due to many different causes. The immature infant has a poor or non-existent sucking reflex. A severe general infection could be another cause. Disturbances of the central nervous system may also impair the sucking reflex. In neonatal tetanus the spasm of the chewing muscles usually results in inability to suck.

Apnoeic spells are common in very immature infants but may also indicate the presence of a central nervous disorder caused by septicaemia meningitis or hypoglycaemia.

Abnormal crying, usually a high-pitched and monotonous cry, is a symptom characteristic of severe central nervous function impairment.

Asymmetric movements of the arms will usually be seen after complicated deliveries such as breech presentations, with difficulties in releasing the arms. The cause is damage to the neural plexus in the neck. There is, in most cases, some ability to move the hand. The symptoms will normally disappear within a few months and recovery will be facilitated if the infant is stimulated to move the arm.

Opisthotonic posture: The infant lies continually in a backward stretched position. The cause is usually severe brain damage, neonatal tetanus, kernicterus or meningitis. A lumbar puncture must be performed to rule out meningitis. The condition is serious and the prognosis poor.

Floppiness or irritability is a non-specific central nervous function impairment and may be due to drugs, given to the mother, an invasive infection, asphyxia or hypoglycaemia.

Jittery movements have the same speed in both directions – both in flexion and extension. They are typical symptoms of immaturity of the central nervous system and should thus be regarded as normal. Pathological convulsive movements usually take the form of one fast and one slow phase of each jerk.

Subtle seizures: such convulsions consist of repeated tonic movements of the eye and/or cycling movements of the legs. Other types of stereotype movements may be present. Subtle seizures may occur both in pre-term and full-term babies. The cause is usually non-specific impaired brain function.

Clonic convulsions often start 1 or 2 days after birth and consist of twisting clonic flexion movements which usually start in one leg or arm and migrate to the whole body. It is most commonly seen in term infants and is usually due to brain oedema or haemorrhage of the brain after perinatal asphyxia.

In **tonic convulsions** muscular contractions take place, causing stretching of the legs and arms. The condition seems to be painful and sometimes the muscles of the cheeks are involved. This condition is most typically found in neonatal tetany.

Causes

As has already been mentioned, the background to neonatal disturbances of the brain function is often multifactorial. The obstetric history should always be scrutinised and indications of perinatal asphyxia in particular looked for. The possibility of **effects of drugs** given to the mother should also be kept in mind. **Malformations** and **viral infections during pregnancy** may cause abnormal brain development and head size, or impairment of vision or hearing. Severe jaundice with 'kernicterus' is another cause.

Intracranial haemorrhage and **cerebral infections** may be due to asphyxia or birth trauma. They may also appear in immature infants for no obvious reason and may give rise to general weakness or localised symptoms such as focal convulsions, inability to suck or general muscular hypertension.

Infections such as septicaemia and meningitis may result in a general impairment of the activity of the infant; and meningitis also usually gives specific symptoms such as convulsions and a bulging fontanelle. If there is any suspicion of a generalised infection, a cerebral fluid examination should, if possible, be done. If this is not possible antibiotic treatment should be initiated.

The most common individual factor behind convulsions in the newborn is **perinatal asphyxia**. About two-thirds of all cases are caused by asphyxia and these infants run a high risk of developing neurological handicaps. **Hypoglycaemia** and **hypocalcaemia** are other causes to be borne in mind. Blood tests should be performed and treatment given where symptoms are present and laboratory results support the diagnosis (see page 99).

Treatment of convulsions

In all cases of neonatal seizures it is important that treatment is given urgently and efficiently so that convulsions disappear – if possible without unduly depressing the central nervous functions of the child.

If specific causes such as hypoglycaemia have been excluded the antiepileptic treatment of convulsions is usually **phenobarbitone.** A single loading dose of 20 mg/kg body weight given subcutaneously and maintenance doses of 7-8 mg/kg body weight per day, divided into two doses, is usually recommended. If phenobarbitone does not control the seizures **diazepam** is given intravenously 1 mg/min in doses of 2-5 mg depending on the size of the baby. An alternative is to give **phenytoin** intravenously in a single dose of 20 mg/kg 1 mg/min, and a maintenance dose of 5 mg/kg per day. There is no proof that prophylactic treatment with phenobarbitone in cases of perinatal asphyxia improves the condition. If convulsions occur treatment should, however, be initiated immediately.

Prognosis

The prognosis of children with neonatal seizures is dependent upon the cause of the condition. An overall estimation is that over 30 per cent of infants will subsequently develop brain damage. Persistent asphyctic convulsions have a very poor prognosis.

Birth trauma

Difficult deliveries may lead to several types of birth trauma – a frequent problem in developing countries.

Subaponeurotic haemorrhage

By subaponeurotic haemorrhage is meant diffuse bleeding in the skull under the skin. The trauma comes after repeated trials with vacuum extraction and the diagnosis is simple. Bleeding is not restricted to the sutures between the bones as in cephalic haematoma, but is instead widespread. In some cases the bleeding may be fatal and blood or a blood substitute must be given due to the resultant severe anaemia.

Fractures of the bones or epiphysiolysis

This is often seen after shoulder dystocia or a breech delivery. The fractured leg is not moved by the baby and the fracture can be palpated easily. The treatment is proper fixation of the fracture for 1 or 2 weeks: the arm should be fixed to the body, the leg is immobilised by hanging it in an extended position, fixed by tape. The position of the fractured bones can be checked by X-ray.

Subcutaneous fat necrosis

This is often seen in the tropics. The cause is not understood but there is an element of trauma involved. The fat necrosis appears some days after birth. The skin becomes red and the underlying fat firm and nodulated, sometimes fluctuating. The disorder may be widely distributed on the upper part of the back and gives the impression of an infection. The prognosis is good and the necrosis will disappear within a few weeks.

Congenital malformations

There are no malformations that are specific to the third world and the reader is referred to standard textbooks. The possibility of treating malformations varies enormously and influences all aspects of management of the condition.

FURTHER READING

1. Vulliamy, D.G. *The Newborn Child* 5th edition. Churchill Livingstone: New York, 1982.

2. Philis, A.G.S. *Neonatology: A Practical Guide.* 3rd edition. W.B. Saunders: Philadelphia, London, 1987.

3. Sinclar, J.C., Bracken, M.B. *Effective Care of the Newborn Infant.* Oxford University Press: Oxford, 1992.

REFERENCES

1. Gregory, G.A., Kitterman, J.A., Phibbs, R.H. *et al.* Treatment of the idiopathic respiratory distress syndrome with continuous positive airway pressure. *New England Journal of Medicine* 1971; **284**: 1333-1340.

2. Sterky, G., Melander, L. *Birth-weight Distribution – an Indicator of Social Development.* SAREC report No. 2, Stockholm, 1978.

3. Finnström, O. Studies on maturity in newborn infants. *Acta Paediatrica Scandinavica,* 1977; **66** :601-604.

4. Silverman, W.A. *et al.* The influence of thermal environment upon survival of newly born premature infants. *Pediatrics* 1958; **22**: 876-886.

5. Fardig, J.A. A comparison of skin-to-skin contact and radiant heaters in promoting thermoregulation. *Journal of Nurse-Midwifery* 1980; **25**: 19-28.

6. Sarman, I. and Tunell, R. Providing warmth for preterm babies by a heated water-filled mattress. *Archives of Disease in Childhood* 1989; **64**: 29-33.

7. Norayanan, I. *et al.* The value of human milk in the prevention of infection in the high risk low birth weight infant. *Journal of Pediatrics* 1982; **99**: 496-498.

11

Perinatal Infections

Perinatal infection is one of the main causes of maternal mortality and perinatal infant death. Infection after an illegal abortion is an enormous problem in many parts of the world and is a heavy burden on the health care system. HIV/AIDS is a rapidly growing threat to perinatal health. Post-delivery sepsis is a largely preventable complication that kills many mothers. To the newborn, there is a threat of infection through unhygienic handling after birth, and such infection is often a fatal complication to other conditions such as asphyxia or pre-term birth.

Predisposing factors

The mother

Pregnancy causes a **change in the immune defence system of the mother,** predisposing to certain infections such as malaria. Maternal **malnutrition** and maternal **anaemia** also predispose to infection. Once the **membranes have ruptured,** there is an increased risk of infection ascending into the uterus.

Lesions in the birth canal after delivery are common sites for entry of infection.

Poor sanitation and hygiene, such as lack of clean water, soap and a clean place to give birth, do not improve the situation.

Exposure to **sexually transmitted diseases** (STD), often long before pregnancy, will increase the risk of such infections in mother and child.

Sexual intercourse in the latter phase of pregnancy has been much discussed as a possible factor predisposing to intrauterine infection, even through intact membranes. At least where the cervix has opened somewhat, and hygiene is poor, sexual intercourse appears to increase the risk of ascending infection and thereby the risk of premature rupture of the membranes. Even so it may be unwise to recommend sexual abstinence in the last trimester, particularly in certain cultural settings, where the woman's attempted abstinence, in actual fact, implies significantly increased risk of STDs because the husband is likely to have extramarital sexual contacts.

Immunisation coverage of the mother against, for example, tetanus will determine to what degree the child has specific protection against such infections.

The infant

The full-term, well-nourished, breast-fed, healthy newborn has a good protection against infection during the first few months of life. This is due in part to the antibodies transferred to the infant transplacentally and through the breast-milk. The colonisation of the skin and the intestinal canal of the infant by the bacterial flora of the family is essential for the protective mechanisms of the infant.

The defence mechanisms of **pre-term and/or malnourished children** are poor, however. The risk for them of contracting a serious infection is increased by the fact that they run a high risk of acquiring **asphyxia, hypothermia** and **poor sucking ability**, leading to **starvation** – all factors resulting in impaired defence mechanisms. Such pathological conditions in the new-born period are usually treated with methods that in themselves bear the risk of infecting the infant, e.g. through **umbilical catheterisation, unclean feeding procedures** etc. Overcrowded neonatal units are particularly dangerous places since **cross-contamination** from one infant to another or from staff members to the child is common.

Modes of transmission (Figure 37)

Transplacental infection is one route of entry during pregnancy. Certain viruses infecting the mother (rubella, cytomegalovirus, HIV and hepatitis B) may pass the placenta, while only few bacterial or parasitic infections, such as syphilis, listeria and possibly malaria, pass via this route.

Ascending infections make the birth canal an important route of entry for bacteria or occasionally virus that the mother has in her vagina or cervix.

At birth, a baby may thus carry an infection acquired during pregnancy or while passing through the birth canal.

During and after delivery there is an increased risk of infection of the mother or the infant. It is particularly common that infections are transmitted from hospital staff to the patients by unclean vaginal examination or by unclean examination of the baby after birth. In Europe, puerperal septicaemia seems to have been fairly uncommon until hospital deliveries began in the early 19th century. Following this, however, about 25 per cent of newly-delivered women in hospital died of fulminant infections. Not until the mode of transmission was understood, were **proper routines for handwashing** etc. introduced and the incidence reduced.

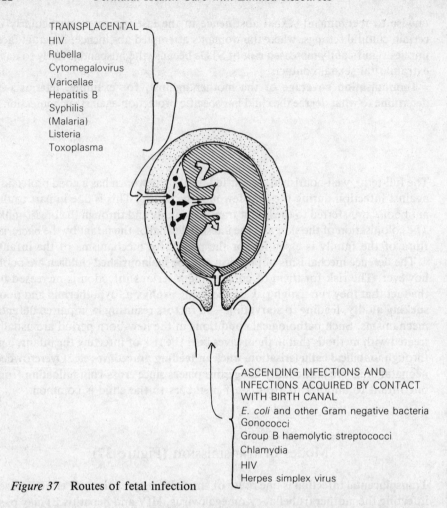

TRANSPLACENTAL
HIV
Rubella
Cytomegalovirus
Varicellae
Hepatitis B
Syphilis
(Malaria)
Listeria
Toxoplasma

ASCENDING INFECTIONS AND
INFECTIONS ACQUIRED BY CONTACT
WITH BIRTH CANAL
E. coli and other Gram negative bacteria
Gonococci
Group B haemolytic streptococci
Chlamydia
HIV
Herpes simplex virus

Figure 37 Routes of fetal infection

But still today, lack of recognition of the importance of handwashing by the staff contributes to the spread of infections. Other measures, such as unnecessary separation of mother and child or care in overcrowded wards, contribute to perinatal infections. Use of overshoes, gowns and other 'hygienic regulations' are often ineffective and expensive, and counteract the establishment of close contact between mother and child.

Unspecific maternal perinatal infections

Amniotic fluid infection syndrome

Around the time of birth there is a danger that **unspecific** infections may attack the mother and child. Such infections are either caused by bacteria that constitute part of the normal vaginal flora or by asymptomatic genital infections in the pregnant woman. 'Amniotic fluid infection syndrome' (AFIS) refers to such a syndrome which combined with inadequate personal hygiene due to lack of water and soap, inadequate housing, nutrition and maternal care seems to explain many pre-term deliveries and perinatal complications. Sexual intercourse at the end of pregnancy also seems to predispose to AFIS, probably due to the trauma to the cervix at intercourse and because the lower membrane pole may be exposed to the vaginal bacteria when the cervical mucus plug has disappeared. While the amniotic fluid normally has antibacterial properties, unfavourable conditions such as those just described may cause a decreased antibacterial activity of the amniotic fluid. This in turn permits invasion of external bacteria, even through intact membranes. AFIS may cause fetal death, premature delivery and above all a child who is highly vulnerable during delivery and shortly after birth. Fetal and neonatal asphyxia are common, as well as serious neonatal infections, due to this unspecific congenital infection syndrome.

MANAGEMENT   Unfortunately AFIS is usually diagnosed after fetal death has taken place, and treatment is seldom possible. Available antibiotics may be tried in case of suspected AFIS. Bacteriological diagnosis should lead to specific antibiotic treatment.

Ascending infections after membrane rupture

Mothers who have had ruptured membranes for a long time before delivery may develop ascending infections of the womb or infecting the neonate. Where the membranes have been ruptured, the term mother should normally give birth within 24 hours to minimise the risk of ascending infection. In situations were the mother has not observed the leakage of amniotic fluid the fetus may be infected for several days before delivery and will have an increased risk of complications and increased mortality during and after birth. Mothers should be taught to be observant as regards possible leakage of amniotic fluid.

CLINICAL SIGNS   While many perinatal infections are associated with a fever, other important infections occur without a rise in temperature. For instance, AFIS often occurs without any rise in temperature. Likewise, ascending infections after ruptured membranes will only cause maternal fever in a late phase. Another sign is foul-smelling amniotic fluid.

MANAGEMENT   Management of manifest ascending infection should include **termination of pregnancy by induction** (oxytocin) and **treatment with antibiotics**. If the mother is in labour oral drugs are resorbed very slowly, and it is preferable to give antibiotics intramuscularly or intravenously.

Puerperal infections

In the puerperium pre-existing pregnancy-related genital infections or insufficient hygiene at delivery may result in puerperal fever and localised **endometritis – myometritis**. If the situation is aggravated a septic condition ('genital sepsis') may occur with potentially fatal bacteraemia.

CLINICAL SIGNS   Clinical signs with full-blown endometritis – myometritis post-partum are high fever, uterine tenderness, foul-smelling vaginal discharge and sometimes expulsion of remnants of membranes or placenta from the uterine cavity.

MANAGEMENT   Management should be a broad-spectrum antibiotic in a sufficiently large **oral** dose, e.g. ampicillin 1 g three times a day. **Drugs such as ergometrine should be avoided unless there is bleeding**, since agents causing the uterus to contract may counteract the blood perfusion and thereby healing of the infected organ.

The prognosis after successful treatment of endometritis – myometritis is good but insufficient treatment may lead to later problems, such as secondary infertility.

Specific maternal and fetal/neonatal infections in the perinatal period

Tetanus

Clostridium tetanii is common in ordinary soil, and is often present in unclean birthing surroundings. The bacteria may rarely lead to maternal infection along the ascending route after delivery. However, the baby may also be infected and neonatal tetanus is, in fact, one of the most common causes of neonatal death in the third world, resulting in about 800,000 deaths each year. The baby is infected at delivery, or during the first days of life. The most important point of entry is the umbilicus.

Good hygiene will diminish the risk of infection but the only way to give the baby full protection is by **immunisation of the mother** twice during pregnancy. The vaccinations should be given with a minimum interval of 3-4 weeks and the final injection given at least 4 weeks before the estimated day of delivery. The maternal antibodies thus developed pass to the fetus and provide protection against tetanus during the first weeks of life. UNICEF has reported that about a third of all pregnant women in very poor countries and about 85 per cent in industrialised countries are fully immunized. There are, however, many women who do not yet receive the second injection and fail to give their child full protection. If the woman also receives a third immunisation against tetanus

6-12 months after the second, she will be protected against tetanus for 5-10 years, and need not be vaccinated if pregnant again during those years.

CLINICAL SIGNS   Inability to suck is the first clinical sign and occurs as a result of trismus (inability to open the mouth due to muscle spasm). This is followed by generalised rigidity and a typical facial expression, with a constant smile (risus sardonicus) and convulsions (Figure 38). An observation only made in neonatal tetanus cases is that it is impossible to open the mouth and examine the throat due to trismus.

MANAGEMENT   Gavage-feeding, sometimes with supplementary intravenous feeding, must be given. Penicillin 100,000 units per kg per day for 5 days is given to eliminate the bacteria. Tetanus antitoxin 5000 units for 3 days is recommended.

Spasms are controlled by paraldehyde 0.3 ml/kg IM or slow intravenous injection of diazepam 1-2 mg/kg. Sedation should be continued during the next days with the use of chlorpromazine 2-3 mg/kg every 6 hours, and phenobarbital 5 mg/kg every 6 hours.

The outcome of neonatal tetanus is influenced by the age of the baby when the symptoms appear, the duration of the spasms, the temperature variation as well as the presence or absence of aspiration pneumonia. The earlier the signs appear, the poorer the prognosis.

In centres where assisted ventilation, curarisation, total parenteral nutrition and good spasmolytic drugs are available the prognosis is good. Unfortunately such centres are rare in those parts of the world where neonatal tetanus is common and the hospital mortality figures are usually 60-80 per cent in such areas.

Malaria

Malaria is a serious blood-borne infection and is becoming increasingly resistant to drugs. The malaria parasite is transmitted between human beings by the

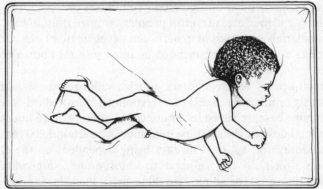

Figure 38   Neonatal tetanus. Stiff muscles in the face, back arms and legs gives the typical posture and appearance of the face.

anopheles mosquito, in which an essential phase of the parasite life cycle also occurs. Areas where malaria transmission occurs all year around are described as holoendemic, and people living in such areas who do not take antimalarials on a regular basis acquire a certain natural resistance to the infection.

The pregnant woman, especially the nulliparous, has a lowered natural resistance to malaria, and often has more frequent attacks during pregnancy. These attacks will render the anaemia more severe and predispose to intrauterine growth retardation. In areas where falciparum malaria is holoendemic, malaria is the single most important cause of pregnancy anaemia. Malaria is also said to be the single most important cause of intrauterine growth retardation throughout the world.

Anaemia is caused by destruction of red blood cells (haemolysis), lack of adequate amounts of folic acid for red cell regeneration, and by general bone marrow depression.

Intrauterine growth retardation is above all caused by placental infestation with subsequent placental dysfunctioning. The placenta appears to function almost as a filter for malaria parasites. In fact, in a pregnant woman with malaria, parasites may be present only in the placenta and not in the peripheral blood, thus causing diagnostic difficulties.

Cerebral malaria may occur during pregnancy, and is an important differential diagnosis in unconscious pregnant women (the other most common possibilities are eclampsia and meningitis).

MANAGEMENT   Malaria **prophylaxis** should ideally be given to all pregnant women throughout pregnancy in areas where malaria is common. The practical dilemmas of such treatment are considerable, however. First, many women make so few antenatal visits that antimalarials given at these visits will be more an intermittent suppression than a prophylaxis. Second, the rapidly changing resistance pattern of malaria creates problems. WHO still favours malaria prophylaxis for pregnant women, in spite of such problems, however. Chloroquine is still the drug usually used for prophylaxis, though others are recommended under certain conditions[1].

In malaria-endemic areas feverish pregnant women must always be **treated** with antimalarials as maternal malaria can never be ruled out. Chloroquine 300 mg once a week is recommended in areas with no known chloroquine resistance.

For treatment of severe malaria attacks, chloroquine should be given intravenously or intramuscularly. The recommended standard dose is 300 mg of chloroquine base, repeated intramuscularly after 8 and 16 hours. In severe cases the total dose of chloroquine base should be around 900 mg in the first 24 hours, dosage on subsequent days being dependent on the effect[2].

In cases which do not respond to chloroquine, sulphadoxine – pyrimethamine (Fansidar) or quinine would be used. Fansidar is given as a single treatment of three tablets. In severe cases, it is combined with oral or parenteral quinine.

None of the above mentioned drugs has any proven teratogenic effect. Fansidar may, however, be allergenic for persons suffering from sulpha allergy.

Congenital malaria has been described but is rare. The majority of the micro-organisms do not pass to the fetus and maternal antibodies pass easily through the placenta and protect the fetus. Malaria organisms have been found in the blood of newborns, which could be due to minor placental transfusions.

Tuberculosis

A pregnant woman with infectious pulmonary tuberculosis may infect her newborn baby shortly after birth and this will be a great danger to the child. It is therefore important to diagnose and start treating a woman with pulmonary tuberculosis during pregnancy.

During antenatal care **women with a cough** lasting more than 3 or 4 weeks should be given extra attention and when suspected of having tuberculosis, be sent for sputum microscopy and, if possible, X-ray examination.

MANAGEMENT   The management is normally a combination of streptomycin injections and oral isoniazid + PAS, or isoniazid + thiacetazone. Streptomycin may cause light to moderate hearing damage in as many as one in six of the babies, however, and the above regimen should therefore be modified where other alternatives are available.

As early as 2 weeks after the start of antituberculotic treatment the risk is only minor that the patient will infect others with tuberculosis. However the treatment must be continued for 6 to 12 months (in accordance with local programmes) for the cure to be complete. Just a few weeks after the initiation of the treatment the woman will no longer run the risk of infecting her child.

If pulmonary tuberculosis is diagnosed at the time of birth the pregnant woman should be treated according to the standard treatment. The new-born baby should also receive isoniazid syrup prophylaxis, dose 4 mg/kg per day and be vaccinated against tuberculosis. Breast-feeding should always be encouraged and the mother and child must not be separated in such cases.

An increasing proportion of people with pulmonary tuberculosis are also HIV infected.

It is very rare for the infant to have been infected by tuberculosis in the womb. In such cases, the clinical picture may resemble that of respiratory distress. Most commonly the child will be infected by transmission from the mother after birth. Symptoms will usually occur during the second or third month after birth. The disease will often be serious and the infant may develop miliary tuberculosis or meningitis.

Syphilis

Maternal syphilis may cause **spontaneous abortion, fetal death,** or **manifest or latent congenital syphilis** in the liveborn. Together with other sexually transmitted diseases, syphilis is a growing problem especially in urban areas. Many African cities have a high annual incidence of this disease.

DIAGNOSIS   Where syphilis is common, maternal screening should be carried out during pregnancy[3], using for instance the RPR (Rapid Plasma Reagin) test. This is a reasonably cheap unspecific serum analysis which is easily performed in a laboratory. The RPR test rarely results in a false negative answer, but about a third of positive results are false. Therefore the diagnosis should, if possible, be confirmed by more specific methods.

CONGENITAL SYPHILIS   If the mother is not treated during pregnancy there will be considerable risk of abortion or stillbirth. The infant may, however, appear quite healthy at birth. Liveborn infants may have manifest or latent congenital syphilis. When infection is manifest the baby may be acutely ill with pyrexia, desquamated eruptions on palms and soles (red and swollen) and enlargement of liver and spleen. During the coming days rhinitis, jaundice and anaemia may develop. However, babies may also appear perfectly well at birth, however, and only slowly develop syphilis symptoms during the first months or years of life. The symptoms will then be more similar to those of secondary syphilis in adults – skin eruptions and characteristic dental, or skeletal problems. Sometimes the presenting symptom is a pseudoparalysis of an arm or leg. This is caused by the pain originating from an osteo-chondritis, which is usually easily shown up on an X-ray picture. This wide range of effects of syphilis infection reflects the fact that syphilis is a systemic infection with endarteritis as its local manifestation.

Serological tests are of little value in the newborn. At birth the antibody levels of the mother and the offspring will be approximately the same. If the mother has been treated before birth the only mean to prove diagnosis in an asymptomatic newborn is by repeated serological tests or by the expensive specific Immunoglobin M (IgM) titre assessment.

MANAGEMENT   Seropositive mothers and their partners should be treated with penicillin during pregnancy to avoid congenital syphilis. The most common treatment of the mother is a single dose of 2.4 million units of benzathine benzylpenicillin in two portions. This is a cheap and simple way of acquiring the long duration penicillin level needed to eradicate the infection. Other treatment alternatives are possible but must be extended to 15-17 days. Shorter antibiotic treatments – for instance against other infections – may cure syphilitic symptoms, but will leave a latent infection. Syphilis has shown no signs of resistance to penicillin.

The infant with congenital syphilis should be given benzathine benzyl-penicillin, one injection of 900,000 units or repeated injections over 2 weeks.

All symptomatic cases should be treated with penicillin. In most parts of the world asymptomatic offspring of seropositive mothers are also commonly given penicillin. Another option is to follow the infants as described above. In such cases there is a risk that the child may be lost in the follow-up, indicating that treatment could also be rational in infants with no clinical signs.

Gonorrhoea

Gonorrhoea is also a sexually transmitted disease (STD) that may be present without any symptoms at all. The risk of transmission to the baby at the time of birth is high and many of the infected babies will develop gonococcal conjunctivitis in the neonatal period.

DIAGNOSIS   If vaginal discharge or dysuria is present in a pregnant woman a clinical examination including, if possible, microscopy with Gram stain of the discharge, should be performed. The oxidase test verifies the presence of *Gonococcus* bacteria detected in the Gram stain. A bacteriological culture is rarely available, *Gonococcus* also being highly sensitive to transport.

NEONATAL GONORRHOEA   The symptoms of gonorrhoea in a newborn infant are usually limited to the eyes. A purulent **conjunctivitis** will occur and, in serious cases, the infection will within a few days have developed into a keratitis and a deep inflammation of the tissues of the eye. In such cases, sight will be lost in the affected eye.

MANAGEMENT   Maternal gonorrhoea is commonly treated by 3.5 grams of oral ampicillin given together with 1 gram of oral probenecid to delay renal clearance of penicillin given. Procaine penicillin has also been used, but is today largely discarded as a method due to increasing problems of bacteriological resistance. New drug regimens have therefore been developed. Poor patient compliance, inadequate self-prescribed treatment, and repeated re-infections contribute to the spread of multiresistant gonococci.

OPHTHALMIA NEONATORUM   is partly prevented by the routine instillation of 1 per cent silver nitrate in both eyes immediately after birth. This procedure is recommended in all countries where gonorrhoea is common. If a gonorrhoidal ophthalmia is developing, penicillin eye drops and intramuscular injections of ampicillin should be given.

AIDS in adults

EPIDEMIOLOGY   Acquired immune deficiency syndrome (AIDS) constitutes a rapidly increasing problem in the world. Since the first case of AIDS was diagnosed in 1981, the virus causing the disease, human immunodeficiency virus or HIV, has rapidly spread all over the world. In December 1992,

30 per cent of pregnant women in certain Africans cities were infected with HIV, and Latin America and South-east Asia report rapidly growing infection rates. The next decade will see many millions of people dying of AIDS, and large numbers of children will be left without parents as a result of AIDS. The risks to children in the future must therefore be particularly stressed in public education programmes on AIDS.

CLINICAL SIGNS   A wide variety of infections attack the HIV-infected person as a result of lowered immune defence mechanisms. Skin infections, infections of the mouth, pulmonary tuberculosis, pyelonephritis, herpes zoster and deep purulent tissue infections are examples. Loss of weight and spells of sweating are also common.

DIAGNOSIS   The clinical picture together with a positive serological screen test give a probable diagnosis of HIV infection. If available, a confirmatory test will ascertain the diagnosis.

AIDS in new-born babies

EPIDEMIOLOGICAL ASPECTS   Studies from different parts of the sub-Saharan region have shown that 30-50 per cent of the infants from infected mothers are infected with the virus at birth. In Europe and USA the figure is 20-30 per cent. It has also been demonstrated that the virus may pass into the mother's breast-milk and cause seroconversion in the baby. Breast-feeding is still recommended by WHO – even when the mother carries the infection. The advantages of breast-feeding are considered to outweigh the risk of transmission via the mother's milk.

CLINICAL SIGNS   At birth most HIV-infected infants are growth-retarded but otherwise free of symptoms. Within the first six months of life more than half of the infected infants will have become ill and within the first 5-6 years the vast majority of the infected infants will have clinical signs of the disease in the form of continued growth retardation and retarded psychomotor development as well as other signs of central nervous system involvement, e.g. cerebral palsy. The growth retardation is exaggerated by chronic diarrhoea and malnutrition. In many infants a typical chronic infection of the parotid glands occurs. Early invasive infections with bacterial septicaemia, meningitis and pneumonia are common. Opportunistic infections, well-known from adult cases of AIDS, are late symptoms in infants. On clinical examination enlarged lymph glands, liver and spleen will often be found. X-ray of the lungs often shows a typical LIP (lymphoid interstitial pneumonitis) picture with interstitial infiltrations and enlarged lymph glands.

DIAGNOSIS   Laboratory tests will show low levels of red and white blood cells and platelets. Since the HIV antibodies are transferred from the mother to the baby it is impossible to determine whether or not the baby is infected at birth[4]. Not until the age of 3-4 months will the maternal antibodies have disappeared. It is then possible to follow the antibody production of the child. However, some infected infants may start producing measurable antibodies at a later date. When the mother is HIV positive it is thus not possible to exclude congenital HIV infection until the age of about 18 months.

MANAGEMENT   There is at present no treatment providing a cure for HIV infection. All HIV infected new-born infants will sooner or later develop AIDS and die, usually within the first few years of life. Treatment with acyclovir (AZT), large doses of gammaglobulin and intensive anti-biotic treatment in case of bacterial infection, may prolong life. There are rare reports of children surviving into the teens. In a society with limited economic resources the tremendous costs for treatment of infected infants must be weighed against investing the same amount of money in programmes to prevent the spread of the disease, e.g. by informing students, mass media campaigns and other means of making society aware of the AIDS threat to the new generation and the possibilities of limiting the epidemic.

Control of the spread of HIV

Organisation of HIV testing, confirmation of positive HIV screening tests and of counselling, perhaps also with the inclusion of legal abortions for HIV positive women, is extremely difficult in many developing countries. Serological testing for HIV is complicated by the presence of two types of HIV, at least in Africa. Testing for HIV in such regions at present requires two different tests. Present HIV screening tests combine high sensitivity with high specificity, however. Thus, a positive HIV screen test has a high predictive value for HIV infection, at least in areas where HIV prevalence is high.

A special problem is the risk of infection of delivery room staff. In most large labour units of the world, the risk of being infected with HIV from handling the blood of infected women is a continuous threat. Supervising staff face a great challenge in combatting a general staff AIDS panic, through detailed information and instruction. Fortunately, HIV is not highly contagious as is, for instance, hepatitis B, and it does not readily transverse intact skin. Contact between parturients' blood and body entries of delivery room staff – wounded skin, bruises, cuts or eyes – should be avoided. Gloves, protective spectacles and a correct 'no-touch' technique of suturing should be adopted. The traditional way of digitally locating the needle when suturing tears must, for instance, be discarded. Rules of skin cleaning and disinfection must be familiar to all staff, and disinfectants must be available. A cheap and effective disinfectant is sodium hypochlorite (bleach).

Hepatitis B

EPIDEMIOLOGY   It is calculated that 200 million people in the world are carriers of this virus. In parts of Asia the carrier rate is as high as 15 per cent of the population. The transmission of the virus from mother to child and early infection after birth contribute to making this infection a great health problem in these parts of the world. The transmission rate from mother to child differs between different ethnic groups: in Taiwan the transmission rate is 40 per cent while in other parts of the world the rate is only one tenth of that level. The highest risk of transmission occurs if the mother acquires the primary infection in the last trimester of pregnancy.

DIAGNOSIS AND MANAGEMENT   There are few adult patients with clear-cut symptoms of primary hepatitis B infection. Serological tests such as hepatitis B surface antigen (HBsAg) are therefore the markers most frequently used in diagnosis. In endemic areas this test may be included in antenatal screening if it is possible to give the baby treatment at birth. The treatment consists of 200 mg hepatitis B immunoglobulin IM and 0.5 ml (10 μg) hepatitis B virus vaccine at birth. The vaccination is repeated 1 month and 6 months after birth[5].

Due to the high cost of the serological test, the immunoglobulin and the vaccine, most developing countries cannot afford such a programme. The result is that the infants will be chronic carriers of the disease and a small number will develop fulminant liver disease with necrosis. The infected infants also have an increased risk of liver carcinoma in adult life. They continue to be a source of risk of transmission of this very contagious infection to other people in the future.

Other specific infections

Rubella, toxoplasmosis, herpes simplex type II, group B streptococci, *Listeria* and *Chlamydia* are other specific infections of perinatal interest. In developing countries they may not be readily diagnosed and they are there presumably overshadowed by the infections already mentioned. The reader is referred to standard textbooks concerning such infections.

Clinical picture of infections in the newborn

Skin infections

Skin infections and umbilical infections may easily occur if the infant's skin is contaminated by virulent bacilli. These may be transmitted from the birth canal of the mother, from the nursing staff or from contaminated soil etc. Lesions, wounds and particularly vulnerable sites like the umbilicus or the edge of the nails, may be the entry point of the infection. The most common causative agent is *Staphylococcus*. In cases of purulent skin infection a bacteriological diagnosis should preferably be established.

MANAGEMENT   Most cases of skin infection and umbilical infection can be prevented by **good general hygiene, careful treatment of the cord** and strict **handwashing** routines. Topical treatment with antibiotic solutions and – in moderate or severe cases – systemic antibiotic therapy are used once the clinical symptoms have become overt. Even minor skin infections must be treated carefully since they may become more serious and ultimately develop into bacteraemia. Another complication, seen in malnourished and hypothermic infants in poor general condition, is involvement of the deeper skin layers with necrosis and permanent tissue destruction. At clinics and hospitals there is always a risk of epidemic spread of infection to other infants by the hands of the nursing staff or by infected wounds.

Conjunctivitis

During the first few days of life, in particular if silvernitrate prophylaxis has been given, an inflammatory reaction of the eyes is present. Purulent infection must be suspected if the discharge becomes thicker and the swelling and reddishness grow worse. Such purulent discharge is usually caused by gonococci, staphylococci, or chlamydia trachomatis. *Gonococcus* infection usually becomes manifest during the first days after birth, *Staphylococcus* conjunctivitis within about a week and *Chlamydia* slightly later.

MANAGEMENT   Preventive measures comprise good general hygiene and silver nitrate drops in the eyes to prohibit gonorrhoeal conjunctivitis. Treatment of conjunctivitis comprises antibiotic eye ointment (Figure 39) and – in severe cases – parenteral antibiotic treatment. If untreated, chronic inflammation may occur, ultimately resulting in conjunctival and corneal destruction and blindness.

Bacteraemia in the newborn

Bacteraemia may be present without any signs of disease or may be **symptomatic (septicaemia, sepsis).** The presence of bacteria in the bloodstream may lead to a localised infection in the skeleton **(osteitis)**, meningeal membranes **(meningitis)**, joints **(arthritis)**, kidneys **(pyelonephritis)** or the neural synapses **(neonatal tetanus)**. The entry point of the infection may have been the umbilicus, the skin, the throat or the lungs.

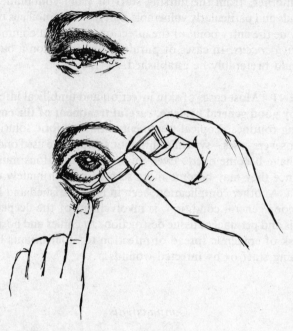

Figure 39   Eye ointment or solution should be applied on the internal
surface of the lower lid of the eye.

Typical symptoms of neonatal septicaemia are respiratory distress and sometimes recurrent apnoea, progressive weakness, hypotonia, refusal to take milk
and grey or pale skin colour.

MANAGEMENT   If possible several blood cultures should be done and
antibiotic treatment, preferably by the intravenous route, should be given
for 7-10 days[6]. Doses are given in Table 7 on page 140. In developing countries
the most common causative agents are staphylococci, colibacilli, streptococci
group B, and species of salmonella. Once the symptoms have occurred the
prognosis is poor unless accurate antibiotic treatment is given urgently.
If symptoms occur only a short time after birth, the course will usually be
severe.

Meningitis

In the majority of cases of meningitis bacteria have reached the central nervous
system through the bloodstream. The pattern of infectious agents thus resembles
that of symptomatic bacteraemia. The clinical signs are increased intracranial
pressure with a tense fontanelle, opistotonus stature, convulsions, raised body
temperature, lethargy, poor feeding and/or vomiting. In the early stages of the

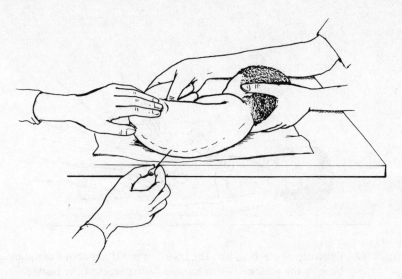

Figure 40 Lumbar puncture in a newborn baby. Note the position,
supported by the attendant, and the angle of the needle.

disease fewer than half the cases will present specific central nervous
symptoms such as convulsions. Since the clinical picture may be very general
it is wise to suspect neonatal meningitis in all cases of severe disease in a new-born
child.

MANAGEMENT   A lumbar puncture (Figure 40) and analysis of the cerebro-
spinal fluid should be carried out. Intravenous antibiotic treatment should
be given in high doses.

Pyelonephritis

The symptoms of pyelonephritis are either an acute septic infection or a more
silent chronic infection. In the acute septic infection the symptoms resemble
that of symptomatic bacteraemia. In the chronic infection the symptoms are
more vague and failure to thrive is often the most prominent sign. Diagnosis
is established by analysis of the urine obtained by a direct puncture of the bladder
(Figure 41).

MANAGEMENT   In the septic type, intravenous antibiotic treatment with the
same antibiotic drugs as in bacteraemia should be used. In the chronic type
ampicillin treatment is often used initially.

Figure 41   Puncture of the bladder. The insertion is 1-2 cm above the pubis
bone in the midline. When the needle has reached the bladder
some urine is drawn into the syringe.

Osteomyelitis

Bone infection is a frequent consequence of bacteraemia in developing countries.
The disappearance of active movements of a leg is a typical clinical sign. If the leg
is moved passively there are clear signs of pain. The differential diagnosis is
mainly against a traumatic fracture or epiphysiolysis. In the latter condition the
symptoms are already present at birth. In osteomyelitis local swelling and redness
are seldom seen, and the X-ray changes may not appear until after several days.

MANAGEMENT   Treatment must be started even where there are no X-ray
findings. Treatment comprises a combination of surgical drainage of the
affected site and intravenous antibiotic treatment during the subsequent weeks.
Antibiotic treatment must be continued for 6 weeks. Even with this treatment
there is a high risk of persistent damage to the affected joint, and disturbed
growth is often seen on follow-up.

Pneumonia

Pneumonia in the new-born baby may be transferred from the mother before
birth. In other cases the cause may be the swallowing of infected material from
the birth canal or infection after delivery. The bacilli can reach the lungs via
the bloodstream or through the throat. Whatever the cause, the infant will
present respiratory difficulties and general weakness, depending on the extent
of the infection.

MANAGEMENT   A chest X-ray is necessary for the verification of the diagnosis. Antibiotics and, if necessary, oxygen, should be given if pneumonia is suspected.

Gastroenteritis

Diarrhoea in the newborn is frequently caused by a bacterial infection, most often by *Salmonella, Shigella, Escherichia coli, Klebsiella* or other pathogens. The source is usually contaminated equipment such as feeding bottles or infected water. The infection is easily spread from one baby to another via the hands of the staff in a nursery. The clinical picture is often severe, particularly in infants who have acquired the infection from the mother during delivery.

MANAGEMENT   It is extremely important that intensive treatment is initiated early and that the salt and fluid balance is supervised. The best way of preventing diarrhoea is breast-feeding, which should also be maintained where symptoms are present.

Prevention of perinatal infections

Pregnant women

Ways of reducing the risk of perinatal infection can be deduced in part from what has already been said.

Sexual spread must be emphasised by doctors and other health staff as a major threat to perinatal well-being. The world is facing the enormous threat of AIDS and obstetricians, paediatricians, all other medical staff and health authorities at all levels must be quite clear about the HIV/AIDS message: mutual faithfulness is the only safe principle today, otherwise, reduce the number of contacts and use a condom. A safe sexual behaviour will also decrease the risk of contracting other STDs which will in turn diminish the risk of having an infected baby or becoming sterile. Such information should be provided, taking cultural sensitivities into consideration, at schools, military camps, STD clinics and by mass media.

Improving maternal nutrition and organising **maternal immunisation against tetanus** are also important issues and should be facilitated by community leaders and health authorities.

Basic obstetric services to **care for women with membrane rupture** without contractions, or with prolonged labour are other important measures for prevention of perinatal infections.

During and immediately after delivery the most important aim is to avoid pathogens being allowed to occupy the mucous membranes or sore areas of the genital tract of the mother or the newborn baby. To achieve this the birth site must be kept clean. Before touching the baby or the genital tract of the mother the hands of the attendant must be washed with water and soap. Instruments, clamps etc. should be boiled before use or, preferably, sterilized. Special attention must be paid to the treatment of the umbilical cord (see Chapter 4).

The new-born baby

Since it is well known that the newborn baby will easily acquire infections, rigorous hygiene routines are practised in many maternity wards and wards for the newborn. Most of these routines, such as slip-on shoe covers, face masks and caps, are ineffective and have a negative impact on care of the mother and infant. They are also costly. The most dangerous source of infections is the hands of the staff. Consequently, hand washing is the most important method for combatting infections. Hands must be washed **before clean** and **after dirty** activities. Separation of the infant from the mother in order to avoid infection is never to be recommended. Only one infant should be put in each bed or incubator (if needed) in order to avoid cross-contamination.

The aim of neonatal care is for the newborn baby to be colonised with the same bacteria as the mother and to avoid colonisation with hospital bacteria. The latter are often penicillin-resistant *Klebsiella, Pseudomonas* and *Staphylococci*. Thus **a rooming-in system,** keeping the mother and child together, is to be preferred to care of mother and child in separate rooms. The close contact with the mother promotes **breast-feeding**. In many developing countries breast-feeding is a pre-condition for survival. Successful breast-feeding on leaving the hospital is thus the most important prophylactic measure for reducing the risk of future infection in the neonate. Breast-feeding must also be maintained with sick and pre-term babies.

It is advisable to **reduce the number of visitors** to the baby during the first week of life. This is particularly important if the persons concerned carry an infection. Members of staff should not assist with nursing care if they have flu or infected wounds on their hands.

For routine care these simple rules are enough. If more advanced technology is used the risk of infecting the child will increase.

Avoid invasive methods if possible: do not use suction on the babies unless necessary. If you have to use suction, do it carefully and for short periods. If a pump is used, use a T-tube and suck at intervals.

Do not use endotracheal tubes unless necessary. Instead, use a bag and mask.

Do not use intravenous or intra-arterial catheters unless necessary. If a child is treated with a respirator then endotracheal intubation and umbilical artery catheterisation will be included in the treatment though this is a rare situation in developing countries.

If the gastrointestinal tract can be used for nutrition this is to be preferred to intravenous nutrition. Necrotising enterocolitis or intestinal malformations requiring surgery are conditions which necessitate intravenous nutrition.

If possible **avoid putting more than one baby in each incubator**. In such situations it is better to use the mother as a source of heat. In incubators, the humidifying system implies a risk of contamination of the baby. It must be cleaned properly and the water replaced regularly. A solution with silver nitrate will protect the water from multiplication of germs which otherwise will start within 1 or 2 days.

Tools and instruments used in care, such as forceps, tubes and face masks, must be cleaned carefully and **sterilised with boiling water** for 20 min before use.

In neonatal care units **separate gowns should**, if possible, be used for the care of the different infants. This means that the doctor or nurse must change the gown before and after taking care of each individual infant.

Management and antibiotic treatment

Early treatment with antibiotic drugs is of vital importance whenever a serious infection is suspected. It is thus not possible to wait for the results of different laboratory examinations. The treatment must initially be determined by the clinical signs revealed on physical examination. Since infections in new-born babies may rapidly become serious early treatment is very important. On the other hand antibiotics should not be used where not justified. Antibiotics are usually expensive and excessive use will sooner or later result in the appearance of resistant strains. We suggest the following guide-lines for initiating antibiotic treatment in a baby just admitted to a neonatal unit.

1. Antibiotics should be given if the **medical history** shows:

    ● that the mother had signs of amniotic fluid infection;

    ● that the interval between the rupture of the membranes and delivery was more than 24 hours;

    ● that the infant has been asphyctic and been resuscitated, particularly if there has been meconium stained amniotic fluid.

2. Antibiotics should also be given if the baby shows any of the following **symptoms or signs:**

    ● body temperature below 35°C or above 37.5°C;

    ● respiratory difficulties;

    ● distended abdomen;

    ● tense fontanelle;

    ● apnoeic spells;

    ● feeding problems with no obvious reason;

    ● any signs indicating specific infection.

Recommended doses of some frequently used antibiotics are given in Table 7.

3. **General prophylactic treatment should not be practised** either in developing or in industrialised countries.

4. **Antibiotics should not be given after Caesarean section** (in uncomplicated cases), **in uncomplicated pre-term babies or to hyperbilirubinaemic infants** during phototherapy, provided there are no signs of infection.

A blood sample for culture of bacilli should, if possible, be taken before treatment. Our guide-lines will result in the use of antibiotics in some non-infected infants. Thus a certain degree of over-use is recommended for safety reasons. In many instances the treatment could be discontinued if the symptoms disappear and there are no signs of infection.

Apart from medical treatment good nursing care of the baby is essential. This may include regulation of the thermal environment, support observation looking for changes in general condition, apnoea, convulsions or abnormal body temperature.

TABLE 7

Suggested dosage of some antibiotic drugs

| Drug | Total daily dose | Doses per 24 hours | |
		Baby is 0-2 days old	Baby is 3 days to 3 weeks old
Benzylpenicillin	30 mg/kg*	2	3
Ampicillin	50-100 mg/kg	2	3
Gentamicin	2.5 mg/kg	1	2
Cloxacillin	50-100 mg/kg	1	2
Chloramphenicol	12.5-25 mg/kg	2	3
Cefuroxime	7.5-10 mg/kg	2	3

*One mg corresponds to 1500 international units.

Benzylpenicillin or ampicillin combined with an aminoglycoside such as gentamicin have been used successfully in the treatment of unknown bacterial infections. Penicillin has a more narrow spectrum than ampicillin and does not cover *Listeria monocytogenes*. Penicillin has less influence on the gastrointestinal flora than ampicillin. 'Third generation' cephalosporins are effective and are used more and more although they are expensive.

The reason that all antibiotic drugs are given less often during the first days of life is the immaturity of the detoxification system in the liver and kidney in the newborn. After a few days these systems will become more effective and the number of doses can be increased.

FURTHER READING

1. *Maternal and Perinatal Infections.* WHO: Geneva, 1991.

2. Remington, J.S., Kein, J.O. (eds): *Infectious Diseases of the Fetus and Newborn Infant.* W.B. Saunders: Philadelphia, 1990.

3. Crofton, J., Horne, N., Miller, F. *Clinical Tuberculosis.* Macmillan: London and Basingstoke.

REFERENCES

1. Nathwani, D., Currie, P.F., Douglas, J.G. *et al.* Plasmodium falciparum malaria in pregnancy: a review. *British Journal of Obstetrics and Gynaecology* 1992; **99**: 118-24.

2. WHO. Practical chemotherapy of malaria. *WHO Technical Report Series* No. 805. Geneva, 1990.

3. Hira, S.K., Bhat, G.J., Chikamata, D.M. *et al.* Syphilis intervention in pregnancy. Zambian demonstration project. *Genitourinary Medicine* 1990; **66**: 159-64.

4. Mok, J.Q., Giaquin, C., deRossi, A. *et al.* Infants born to mothers seropositive for HIV. *Lancet* 1987; **i**: 1164-7.

5. Xu, Z-Y., Liv, C-B., Francis, D.P. *et al.* Prevention of perinatal acquisition of hepatitis B virus carriage using vaccine. *Pediatrics* 1985; **76**: 713-18.

6. Vesikari, T., Janas, M., Grönroos, D. *et al.* Neonatal septicemia. *Archives of Disease in Childhood* 1985; **60**: 542-6.

12

Organisation of Perinatal Care

Preventive perinatal health care assumes that it is possible to foresee and predict certain complications of pregnancy and delivery. In addition, some maternal risk factors that are associated with an adverse pregnancy outcome for both the mother and the baby (e.g. short stature, previous Caesarean section, limp leg) are relevant in all subsequent pregnancies, and a longitudinal perspective is therefore useful.

It is important to emphasise that **preventive** health measures include **pre-pregnancy interventions**, such as sexual education and contraception counselling. A longitudinal perspective on maternal care means that pregnancies and intervals between pregnancies are looked upon as links in the chain of reproductive life. **Preventive antenatal care** should constitute the basis for **preventive delivery care** and they should be organically linked together.

A key issue in the organisation of perinatal care is good preventive delivery care. The organisation of delivery care will therefore be given emphasis in this section. Another fundamental part of this section concerns the documentation of delivery care. The basis of such documentation is the patient's record, the quality of which will be given particular attention.

If manpower resources are scarce a careful discussion of the professional responsibility is necessary and there should be active delegation to achieve an optimal staff utilisation.

More than half of all deliveries in the world are home deliveries, unattended by trained staff. These deliveries take place under poor conditions, but most of them occur without complications. Improving the quality of **home deliveries** is extremely important in third world obstetrics to reduce maternal mortality and perinatal infant mortality. The first objective must be to create conditions for **'the hygienic home delivery'**, compatible with the **'three cleans': clean hands, clean perineum, and clean cord care** (China).

The setting and its actors

About 80 per cent of all childbirths take place in the developing world. More than half of them take place at home. Few women give birth totally alone. Local women with their own varied experience assist at the delivery. These women are called traditional birth attendants (TBAs) (Figure 42).

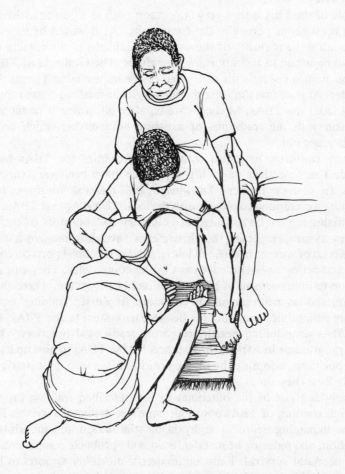

Figure 42   Traditional midwives, also called traditional birth attendants (TBAs) assist a large proportion of all deliveries in the developing world. This will continue to be so, and TBAs must therefore be used fully.

Traditional birth attendants (TBAs)

The TBA is often an older woman who has gone through childbirth many times herself. She has learned to assist at childbirths from other local women and perhaps she comes from a line of TBAs. She may give traditional treatments during pregnancy, or prescribe certain behaviour in accordance with culture and tradition. The TBA is usually illiterate and has no formal health education. She shares the beliefs and traditions of the women who are giving birth. Being culturally competent, she has a natural capacity to support and give comfort to the birthing woman and her family. She often has a certain social status and prestige in the community in which she is working. Being a TBA is usually a part-time occupation: payment is received after completion of the delivery.

The role of the TBA is thus very important, both as a person assisting births and as a prestigeous person in the community. As it would be impossible to institutionalize the majority of the world's childbirths in the coming decades, TBAs will continue to be important care givers. The vital role of TBAs gives rise to the question of how the care given can be improved and home deliveries made safer. At the same time one should ask, if the medical system could learn anything from the TBAs. Medical care is, after all, a recent phenomenon in comparison with the traditions of assisting homebirths, which are several thousand years old.

In many countries or areas, training programmes for TBAs have been launched. The objectives of such programmes have been very varied, from attempts to convey medical knowledge and medical routines, to solely maintaining a continuous dialogue with the local TBAs. At best TBAs, through fruitful dialogue, can be recruited as voluntary collaborators of the primary health-care system, respecting the 'three cleans', avoiding dangerous treatment, timely referral of women in difficult labour, giving regular reports on childbirths assisted and acting as health educators in the community. They can also give inspiration to improvement of institutionalised birthing care, where alienation, separation and isolation are all too common. At worst, 'training' can signify a one-way communication from the health-care system to the TBAs, resulting in the TBAs abandoning health-promoting traditional practices. One TBA training programme in Africa, for instance, led the TBAs to give up traditional birthing positions, adopting the supine position often seen in obstetric practice – 'that is how they do in hospital'.

Critically analysis of the outcomes of the described training programmes reveals that training of TBAs above all improves neonatal survival. Reducing heat loss, managing neonatal asphyxia by stimulation and mouth-to-mouth resuscitation, and reducing neonatal infections are probable components of these gains in neonatal survival. Reducing maternal mortality appears to be much more difficult. This may be because maternal complications often are sudden and unexpected – eclampsia, or profuse post-delivery haemorrhage for instance – and because the TBA in such situations can do very little. Cost-effectiveness analyses indicate that significant reduction of maternal mortality is better achieved by training more midwives and making basic institutional birthing care more accessible, than by TBA training programmes.

The conclusion thus appears to be, that TBAs will continue to be active in the world for many years to come, that the main benefits of locally adapted TBA training programmes is in the improvement of child survival, that institutional birthing care often has something to learn from TBAs, and that 'TBA training programmes' therefore should be based on dialogue.

Midwives and nurses

Trained nurse-midwives are the backbone of modern perinatal care. Some countries recognised the need to train midwives quite late, but today practically all countries of the world have midwifery education. It has been shown in developed countries that the development of national midwifery coverage has often been the single most important measure in reducing maternal mortality.

However, it is difficult to achieve a national coverage of midwives. Inadequate numbers of trained midwives, or difficulties in employing existing midwives are further challenges. They are often badly paid for long working hours. Midwives in health posts and health centres often work without regular contact with the local hospital, often also without sufficient drugs and equipment.

Midwives may serve independently in ordinary **antenatal care**, usually without support from doctors. Overburdened antenatal clinics constitute a demanding challenge. The need for encouragement, feedback, and re-training is great. Providers of antenatal care (midwives) and consumers (pregnant women) are increasingly in need of improved quality of antenatal care. The setting should provide such co-ordination of midwifery care that the pregnancy outcome for the mother and baby really (and not only seemingly) improves.

Midwives also play a key role in **delivery care**, their traditional task. Giving emphasis to safe motherhood and to safe birth, the setting will undoubtedly demand more obstetric skills from home delivery care midwives, much like the pattern in many affluent countries, where midwives have taken over several tasks conventionally carried out by doctors. On the other hand, nurses-midwives in several developing countries (more than in developed countries) have to take over some of the doctors' tasks (minor surgery, tubal ligation, legal abortions, and even Caesarean sections) due to the unavailability of doctors in rural areas. They should then be carefully trained for such interventions.

Medical assistants

Between the level of nurse-midwife and doctor many countries have trained a staff category that is often unknown in the developed world, named e.g. medical assistant or clinical officer. These individuals combine superior nursing training with some diagnostic and therapeutic skills and are extremely useful in the third world setting. For instance, a medical assistant is often in charge of a health centre, and he may be the first extra support on whom a midwife can call when in difficulty. Medical assistants sometimes give anaesthesia and operate independently. In some countries they have specialised in surgery ('surgical assistants, técnicos de cirurgia') and have in reality the position of general surgeons.

Doctors

The most peripheral position for doctors in rural areas is usually at the district hospital. Although the varied and heavy burden met at this level is a great challenge, a competent general doctor is often not available but instead a young inexperienced doctor. The latter may be unwillingly stationed there for a fixed period before pursuing a specialised career in an urban area.

Specialised doctors such as obstetricians and paediatricians work only rarely outside the big cities. Increasing urban populations, with higher hospital attendance, tie these specialists to the cities, as do professional (equipment, development) and personal (career, private practice) motives.

Community support

All those involved in perinatal care, non-professionals as well as health professionals, need the back-up from community leaders, politicians, labour and women unions etc, and from the general public. High quality perinatal care cannot be achieved unless there is an understanding of the reproductive life cycle and how it depends on living conditions and health care for women and children. Health professionals have to interact with community members in order to identify problems, set priorities and work out plans[1].

Different levels of perinatal care

Antenatal care

Antenatal care is a prerequisite for better perinatal health. It should consist of **health education, prevention of complications, treatment of common diseases,** and **risk screening/referral.**

In antenatal care pregnant women are introduced to the health care system. This introduction should imply **confidence** and **satisfaction**, which will guarantee a high continuation rate.

Referral of some pregnant women to clinics for high-risk patients is an important function of antenatal care. High risk cases can be managed as both out-patients and in-patients.

Pre-delivery care of high-risk women

The last trimester is characterised by an increasing risk of various complications. Out-patient care of high-risk pregnancies requires more frequent check-ups. A necessary complement to out-patient antenatal care is **in-patient antenatal care**. Several pregnancy complications in the third trimester need periods of observation and treatment in hospital. The importance of in-patient care is best illustrated by the detrimental effect on pregnancy of a heavy daily workload for a poor pregnant woman – carrying water, food, and firewood. An insufficient number of available beds necessitates restrictions regarding in-patient care, but it is often advisable to aim at combining short periods of in-patient care with frequent out-patient check-ups.

There are three different levels of pre-delivery care. The **first level** corresponds to the concept of 'maternal waiting area' (maternal village), not too far from a hospital with a surgical theatre. Selected pregnant women (without overt disease) can be referred either because otherwise they would have to walk a long distance when labour begins, or because of registered risk factors (breech, twins, possible need for Caesarean section, or symphysiotomy, etc). This system is implemented in some African countries and in Cuba. It also satisfies **the need for rest** of the high-risk pregnant woman about a month before the expected day of confinement. It is of utmost value to have a risk pregnancy close to an obstetric facility and to have **rapid access** to qualified delivery care for both high-risk and those low-risk women who live far away from the first referral level.

The **second level** is designed for women, whose pregnancies are complicated by, for instance, pre-eclampsia, pre-term labour, or pre-labour rupture of membranes. Such women require rest and some supervision, e.g. by a midwife or by a nurse, but may not need daily care by a doctor. Wards at this level may be similar to a maternal waiting area but should ideally be supervised by a midwife or by another trained person.

The **third level** caters for more severe cases with bleeding complications, threatened pre-term birth, cervical insufficiency, intrauterine growth retardation, and severe cases of pre-eclampsia. These high-risk wards should be situated close to qualified delivery care with surgical facilities. It is important that the three levels collaborate closely and that a rotation of the patients can be achieved.

Delivery care

Births at home cannot easily be 'organised' in a poor country. It is, however, important to bear in mind that domiciliary births must be increasingly covered by outreach activities that aim at saving lives when unforeseen complications arise during home births. In some countries supervising midwives serve as TBA tutors with the duty of facilitating TBA contacts/referrals to health units. In this sense it is important to include domiciliary births in organization of perinatal care.

Pregnant women, who are classified in antenatal care according to risk, should be similarly classified at delivery in hospital. This is particularly important in overburdened hospitals with little time for due attention to and control of all cases in labour. High-risk cases include mothers with previous Caesarean section, prolonged rupture of membranes, severe pre-eclampsia, suspected low birth-weight fetuses, breech presentation, suspected or verified twins, vaginal bleedings, or cases of suspected previous mechanical dystocia. Infected cases are separated from other patients.

Safe delivery of a baby requires safe **access to surgery**, should complications occur. Of utmost importance is 'the first obstetric aid', given at **'the first referral level'**, usually a district hospital with facilities for surgery, including Caesarean section under local anaesthesia, or symphysiotomy.

Ideally, both facilities should be situated close to the delivery ward to facilitate early intervention. Access to a small surgical theatre and to a blood bank are very important for the delivery ward of such a hospital. Both are needed for the minimum of 5 per cent of an unselected pregnant population that will need a Caesarean section or other surgical interventions.

The blood bank is crucial but also difficult to establish. Blood donors may be difficult to recruit due to local restrictions or cultural inhibitions. Unreliable refrigerators, fear of blood-borne contagious diseases, and local ideas of weakness and impotence after donation of blood may counteract the establishment of a well-functioning blood transfusion service. These restrictions often make it advisable not to consider blood transfusion unless the haemoglobin value is below 60 g/l. One possibility may be to recruit a number of reliable blood donors who live close to the hospital and are willing to give blood with or without incentive. Each such individual then represents a living 'blood bank', who could be called upon when needed.

Each in-patient in a delivery ward must have her own **patient record**. Its character and quality will be crucial for individual patient care and also for further data collection and feed-back and/or follow-up. It should have two features: it should be operational (oriented towards patient care) and optimal for scrutiny (oriented towards collection of relevant data for each individual, mother and new-born baby). A patient's progress in active labour should be recorded on a **partogram**. A modification of the classical partogram has been called a **cervicogram**, since it simply follows the dilatation of the cervix and is oriented towards early observation of deviations in progress of labour. It is described in Chapter 3.

It is also important to use all available information from the **antenatal card**. The maternal health card should have one part for use during antenatal care (the antenatal card), but it should also contain information on delivery events (the delivery card). Ideally it should also contain information on the post-partum and puerperal periods. A good maternal health card should give detailed information on each pregnancy to evaluate pregnancy outcome, child survival, and maternal complications in each contact with the longitudinal maternal health care.

Each delivery ward should have a **delivery ward book**. Even if patient care at

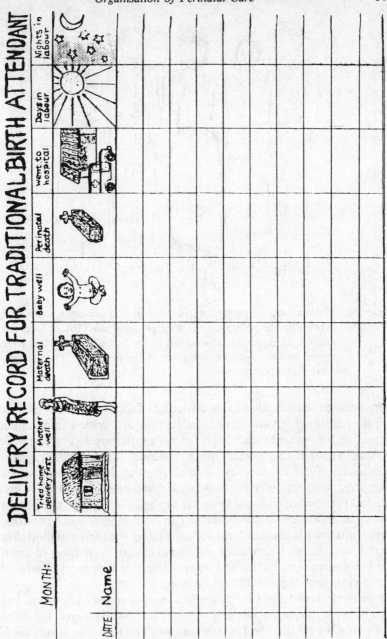

Figure 43 For each month the TBA is supposed to record the dates of
deliveries attended, the names of the mothers and a few pieces of
information on the outcome. The midwife is supposed to check
the cards at her regular visits. The symbols 'Tried home delivery
first', 'Days in labour' and 'Nights in labour' attempt to make
the card action-oriented, telling the TBA when to refer the
labouring woman.

Figure 44   The outcome of pregnancy, for mother and newborn, will largely depend on the assistance she may get from the TBA or local midwife. The doctors and nurses in the hospitals will often have strong influence on the care given in the periphery. The picture symbolises these persons.

delivery must be individualised it is difficult to judge the quality of obstetric care from individual patient records unless they are written so as to allow a retrospective follow-up of each case for review purposes. The status of the delivery ward book is an important quality criterion. It should be comprehensive and completely filled in every day with all relevant details of each delivering woman. Pregnancy outcome for **both mother and newborn** should be given in detail, and the objective should be to lay the basis for forthcoming audit and feed-back to improve obstetric outcome (for both mother and newborn). The delivery ward book is also the basis for calculating the **perinatal mortality rate** at the unit in question. It should be possible to discern the number of low birth-weight babies, pre-term births, and other delivery or pregnancy complications such as twins, breech presentations, eclampsias, etc.

The **delivery record sheet** for home deliveries is equally important but will have to be more simple, particularly if used by TBAs. However, the recording is most useful for guiding the TBAs in their work and for monitoring the births in a community. One example, from Malawi, is shown in Figure 43.

Regular audit sessions with all the staff present are one of the cornerstones of good perinatal care (Figure 44). **Perinatal audit** allows for a careful review of what has happened in a health unit over a certain period (week or month) in order to trace causes of bad outcome of management (perinatal deaths, severe neonatal asphyxia, serious maternal disease and death, etc). It is most important for an audit to be straightforward, honest, and open-minded and to imply constructive criticism of doctors, chief midwives, and other persons in key positions.

In Maputo the mere introduction of a new registration routine in the delivery ward (without any other quality-improving measure in patient care) led to a 30 per cent reduction in the intrapartum death rate for newborns. This indicates that better registration quality will orient the staff towards better patient care. **The staff will find their own performance regularly recorded and made public, a circumstance that leads empirically to better patient care.**

In small health units, as in big hospitals, any improvement in maternal care at delivery starts with a carefully filled-in delivery book. Professional neglect and individual shame should never be allowed to conceal obstetrical mismanagement.

Neonatal care

As was stated in Chapter 4 the most important procedures to be undertaken immediately after birth of a normal baby are to:

● assess the condition of the baby,

● dry him/her,

● cut and clamp the cord,

● keep him/her warm,

● put him/her close to the mother's skin, and

● let him/her suck the mother's breast.

In over 90 per cent of cases these procedures will suffice and the baby can be given to the mother within 2 minutes of birth. When there are no complications the baby can be kept at the mother's breast or in a separate cot. Sucking should be allowed as soon as the baby seems to want to suck. This will stimulate the milk production and most mothers will have milk in their breasts within 2-3 days of the delivery.

The mother and her baby should preferably stay at the health centre or in the hospital for at least 12-24 hours. Before they leave the centre the mother and the baby should be examined by a midwife or a doctor. The observations should be written down in the mother's record. With the deliveries at home the birth attendant should visit the mother and perform a similar examination about 24 hours after delivery.

However, irrespective of place of birth the birth attendant or midwife ought to be prepared to handle a child **who is not breathing at birth**. Unfortunately the procedures to be carried out immediately after birth are too often neglected. Training in basic life support and provision of tools to perform resuscitation are often disregarded.

At least in a hospital an asphyxiated baby needs to be taken care of by two persons: one responsible for cleaning the airways and ventilating the baby, the other for monitoring the heart rate. A separate table for resuscitation should be prepared in advance with equipment for suction, ventilation, heart-rate monitoring and recording of time. To improve the quality of resuscitation procedures is probably the most cost-effective intervention that can be made in most clinics. Recent studies in India and Africa have confirmed that the number of neonatal deaths as well as the number of babies with signs of brain damage after birth will decrease if improved resuscitation procedures are achieved.

Some newborn babies will need additional treatment depending on their condition and available facilities. New-born babies who need further treatment will usually be kept in a separate room or in a separate ward. It is important that this is close to the place where the mother is staying. The facilities have to be arranged to permit close supervision by skilled nurses and to carry out procedures, that may be necessary. The room should have a fairly stable day and night temperature of 22-25°C.

It should be possible to arrange good illumination, and the room should be kept clean and not used for other activities. The number of visitors has to be limited, but the mothers (and their husbands, if possible) should always be permitted to stay with the babies. Clean water, safe electricity, and oxygen supply should preferably be available. All observations, tests performed, and treatments given should be written down in the records with the day, time, and name of the staff member who has written down the note clearly stated.

Puerperal care

Normal, uneventful births in a small health unit or in a hospital often mean a short in-patient period amounting to maximum 24 hours. Complicated deliveries associated with various diseases require a prolonged stay and, hence, a classification of post-partum women according to risk will also be desirable in the puerperal ward. Immediate post-delivery complications are rare in the majority of women while late, sudden bleedings, endometritis, meningitis, malaria, etc., may occur many days or even weeks after delivery, with ensuing risk of maternal death.

Attention should be paid to maternal nutrition, family planning, and maternal health education. The continuity of maternal health care should be emphasized and mothers should be encouraged to return to maternal and child health care clinics after delivery.

How to do it

We believe that more **knowledge** can improve the perinatal health of mothers and children in many countries, without the introduction of more sophisticated equipment such as ultrasound machines, cardiotocographs or ventilators. But how?

The most important thing to do is to put maternal health and women's health in focus. Once the status of women in a society improves, many other things will also begin to improve. It must be repeated many times that healthy babies are born to healthy mothers, and that deprivation of girls and women in a society leads to perinatal problems and perinatal deaths. Repeating this message is the task of everyone: midwives, nurses, doctors, teachers, political groups, decision makers, and others.

Improving the status of women will also give wider acceptance of what a pregnant woman needs:

1. Respect and extra care, including the right not to be overloaded by heavy work during the last part of pregnancy, the right to have enough food to eat, and the right to decide by herself **where** and **how** to give birth. And, against the background of the horrifying maternal mortality caused by clandestine abortions, **if** – in early pregnancy – she wants to give birth.

2. Also the right to be examined at least twice during pregnancy by a well-trained health worker.

3. In a medical institution, the mother has the right to be accompanied during labour, to be treated with respect, to move freely around, and to use the position she prefers at delivery. She should be offered appropriate delivery care by trained and supervised staff.

Procedures that cause resistance to institutional deliveries by making mothers afraid have to be recognised and counteracted (for example routine episiotomies or other surgical procedures, routine enemas, isolation, separation of mother and child, etc.).

In every community, the significance of a well-functioning **preventive care chain** to improve perinatal health should be stressed. It often happens that the few obstetricians and paediatricians, being at the top of the health-care pyramid, have a privileged perspective of the pyramid and therefore a special responsibility in spreading knowledge of this significance. Doctors in general also have the responsibility of supervising and maintaining the perinatal care chain by frequent visits to primary health-care workers and health stations – this is often more important than giving curative care in hospital (Figure 45).

One obstacle to better perinatal health in many parts of the world may be lack of co-operation between obstetricians and paediatricians. All experience shows that a continuous dialogue between the specialised doctors at the top of the pyramid greatly improves perinatal care all the way down to the general population. This book has been written by four specialists, two obstetricians and two paediatricians in that spirit.

Supporting the perinatal care chain means providing education, supervision, and information about the results of work at other levels of the chain, including for instance the very important feed-back to the midwife in the field about

Figure 45   The organisation of perinatal care should include feedback to staff of perinatal audit data (= data from scrutiny of perinatal traumas and deaths – both maternal and fetal/neonatal). This feedback of data is perhaps the most important step for the improvement of perinatal survival through professional and scientifically sound revision of perinatal events and management and evaluation of to what extent traumas and deaths are avoidable. Honest and patient-oriented, critical discussions on a weekly basis help to improve perinatal management.

mothers referred by her to higher levels of care. It also means supporting lower levels in obtaining basic supplies of equipment and medicine.

A serious problem in health care in the third world today is the low status of midwives and nurses. Underpayment or irregular wages often leads to absence from work in order to earn the means of living in other ways. Perinatal care needs staff, and in hospitals there must be staff 24 hours a day. Inexperienced and inadequate staff have little chance of solving the problems of overcrowding, and lack of drugs and equipment. Again, all persons with power, inside or outside the health-care system, must use their power to put the elementary needs of pregnant woman and of those who are giving birth into focus.

Should this book be read by decision makers it is our hope that they will understand that improved perinatal care will decrease maternal and neonatal deaths by at least 90 per cent. There is a need for a change in attitude and in economic support from society and from international organisations so that the recent WHO and UNICEF recommendations on priority for perinatal care can be followed.

Only when more importance is given to the status of women and the improvement of basic preventive care may the goal of a 50 per cent reduction in maternal mortality within 10 years, together with a 50 per cent reduction in neonatal mortality and the eradication of neonatal tetanus within 5 years, be reached. It is our belief that these WHO goals can be reached, provided that the affluent countries offer substantial increases in support and commitment to the deprived and impoverished countries.

FURTHER READING

1. *Essential Elements of Obstetric Care at First Referral Level.* WHO: Geneva, 1991.

2. *Human Resource Development for Maternal Health and Safe Motherhood.* WHO: Geneva, 1990.

3. Cronk, M., Flint, C. *Community Midwifery. A practical guide.* Heineman Medical Books: Oxford, 1989.

REFERENCE

1. Rifkin, S. B. *Community Participation in MCH/FP Programmes.* WHO: Geneva, 1990.

Appendix I: PERINATAL TERMINOLOGY AND DEFINITIONS

The perinatal period

The perinatal period comprises the period from 28 **completed** weeks of gestation to the end of the seventh **completed** day of life.

Birth-weight

The birth-weight is the weight of the newborn infant obtained preferably within 1 hour of birth (before significant post-natal weight loss has occurred). The concept 'low birth-weight' (LBW) refers to a birth-weight of less than 2500 g (that is up to and including 2499 g).

It has been recommended that all fetuses and new-born infants weighing 500 g or more – alive or dead – should be reported in a country's statistics. Obviously, in the developing world, this is not a realistic limit. Hence, WHO has recommended that mortality statistics reported for purposes of international comparison should include only those newborns weighing 1000 g or more (corresponding approximately to 28 weeks of gestation).

Gestational age

The duration of gestation is measured from the first day of the last normal menstrual period. Gestational age should always be expressed in **completed weeks.**

The pre-term period

'Pre-term' refers to 'fewer than 37 completed weeks'. **The concept premature**

is unclear and obsolete in modern perinatal terminology and should not therefore be used. It was previously used as a synonym to LBW but reference should be made **either** to the gestational age **or** to the birth-weight. The concept 'premature' has a functional significance ('before attaining maturity'), which is confusing, since functional maturity at a given gestational age may be difficult to assess and may differ among individual infants.

The term period

This period starts after 37 completed weeks and continues to the end of the 42nd week. It has a duration of 5 full weeks (38-42 weeks).

The post-term period

This period refers to a pregnancy length of more than 42 completed weeks. Sometimes other synonyms are used, e.g. 'post-date' or 'post-mature'. **Post-term** is recommended instead of these synonyms.

Live birth

A live birth has occurred when the new-born infant breathes or shows any other sign of life, such as heartbeat, pulsation in the umbilical cord or movements of the voluntary muscles.

Stillbirth

Stillbirth refers to the birth of a baby showing no sign of life. For international comparisons of perinatal mortality rates only such stillborn infants with a birth-weight of 1000 g or more are included*. Sometimes stillborn babies are not weighed. In this case a gestational age of 28 completed weeks or a body length of 35 cm should be taken as equivalent to 1000 g birthweight. The **stillbirth rate** is defined as the number of stillborn infants per 1000 total births (stillborn infants + liveborn infants).

Early neonatal death

This refers to the death of a liveborn infant during the first 7 days of life. The **early neonatal mortality rate** is defined as the number of early neonatally dead

---

*For national perinatal statistics the Ninth Revision of the International Classification of Diseases (ICD) from 1980 recommends that the lower limit should be 500 g.

infants weighing 1000 g or more occurring 0-7 days after birth, expressed per 1000 livebirths.

Late neonatal death

This refers to the death of a liveborn infant after 7 completed days, but before 28 completed days, after birth.

Perinatal death

Perinatal deaths comprise the sum of all stillbirths and early neonatal deaths. The **perinatal mortality rate** is the sum of all such deaths in relation to the sum of all stillborn and liveborn infants. In other words, it expresses the total fetal/neonatal loss in relation to all infants born (stillborn and liveborn).

Maternal death

A maternal death is defined as the death of a woman while pregnant or within 42 completed days of termination of pregnancy, irrespective of the duration of the pregnancy, from any cause related to or aggravated by the pregnancy or by its management but not due to accidental or incidental causes. There are two main groups of maternal deaths: **direct** and **indirect obstetric deaths. Direct obstetric deaths** result from obstetric complications of pregnancy, labour or puerperium, from interventions, omissions, incorrect treatment or from a chain of events resulting from any of the above. Such diseases comprise e.g. eclampsia, uterine rupture, post-partum endometritis with sepsis or complications following abortions. **Indirect obstetric deaths** are those resulting from previously existing disease or a disease developed during pregnancy and which was not due to direct obstetric causes but aggravated by the physiological effects of pregnancy. Such diseases include diabetes, tuberculosis or heart disease.

The maternal mortality ratio is the number of maternal deaths per 1000 total births. However, the currently most frequently used definition utilises a denominator of '100,000 livebirths'. It is difficult to calculate the total number of births; and the number of liveborn babies is, in practice, an acceptable approximation of the total number of births.

Appendix II: VACUUM EXTRACTION

Instrumental vaginal extraction of the baby, in cephalic presentation, may be by use of either forceps or vacuum extractor.

Safe use of obstetric forceps requires considerable experience of obstetric operations in general and of the use of the instrument itself. Most obstetricians consider that forceps should be used solely by obstetrically trained doctors. During their obstetric training the use of this important instrument should be taught and practised. Therefore it is felt by the authors that this book need not describe this operation. The risks of maternal damage are high if the forceps is used by inexperienced staff, and this cannot be recommended.

Use of the vacuum extractor, on the other hand, carries a low risk of maternal damage even when used by staff with limited obstetric experience. This book thus includes a description of the use of the vacuum extractor, as the procedure may be life-saving for the baby and at times even for the mother, under conditions met in many developing countries. For instance at a distant health centre staffed by midwives, perhaps with the aid of a health assistant or non-obstetrically trained doctor, a vacuum extraction may be a very appropriate procedure. Use in such settings should be taught, trained and promoted.

The vacuum extractor (VE) has several features especially advantageous in labour wards in the developing world. Correctly utilised, the disadvantages are few. It can be used without hurting the mother and, if correctly applied, does not create disproportion or interfere with the normal mechanism of internal rotation. Unlike obstetric forceps, it does not occupy the vital space between the head of the fetus and the wall of the birth canal.

The fact that VE is easy to use without hurting the mother may also lead to its misuse. Misuse often results in failure, sometimes seriously injuring or killing the baby and discredits the method as it is blamed for the bad results. Those who have learned to use the instrument correctly, however, obtain very good results.

Indications

Misuse of VE must be avoided and indications respected. There are four principal indications:

1. **Delay in the pelvic floor phase**. The head has been on or just above the pelvic floor for 60 minutes with full cervical dilatation.

2. **Fetal asphyxia**. Vacuum extraction is not too slow if the instrument is already assembled and the operating vacuum induced rapidly. A prerequisite is that there is no access to rapid Caesarean section and that the fetal head is at least at the spinal level. Symphysiotomy should be considered as an adjunct measure.

3. **Maternal distress**. For termination of the second stage in the case of physical distress, or if an emotionally distressed mother does not respond to customary management.

4. **Extraction of second twin with asphyxia**. Fetal distress in the second twin with cephalic presentation should be managed by VE, also if the head is above the spine. Deflection must be avoided at any price and difficulties in positioning the cup motivate internal version and podalic extraction rather than VE.

Contraindications

All presentations other than cephalic ones are incompatible with the use of VE. Some cephalic positions such as face and brow presentations are also contraindications. It is possible to correct some cephalic deflection positions by positioning the cup close to the small fontanelle.

Technique

Application

An assistant connects the distal end of the suction tube to the vacuum pump. The operator retracts the perineum with one or two fingers, edges the cup into the vagina and firmly pushes it towards the posterior fontanelle. The application distance (see Figure 46) is important for optimum positioning of the cup.

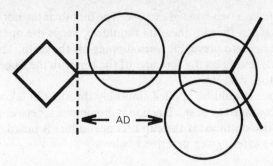

Figure 46   The application distance (AD) between cup edge and posterior
corner of the greater fontanelle is crucial for successful vacuum
extraction, particularly in occiput posterior positions. If the AD
exceeds 3 cm almost all (98 per cent) of occiput posterior
positions will be reversed to occiput anterior ones.

Vacuum

When the cup has been correctly positioned it is pressed against the scalp with
two fingers of one hand while the index finger of the other hand is swept around
the rim of the cup to check that there is no maternal tissue between the rim
and the scalp. A vacuum of 0.2 kp/cm^2 is induced and the cup checked or rechecked for position and possible entrapment of maternal tissue. When the
operator is satisfied with the application the vacuum is increased as rapidly as
possible (in one step) to 0.8 kp/cm^2 or to 0.5 kp/cm^2 if the fetus is pre-term.
It is unnecessary to induce the vacuum slowly, step by step. If a hand pump
is used it should be operated until the head has been extracted.

Extraction

The cup is rechecked and traction is then applied at the onset of the next contraction, in the direction of the pelvic axis, which means downwards if the woman
is lying on her back (Figure 47).

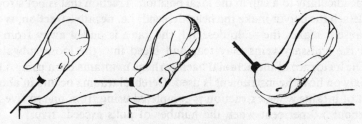

Figure 47   Optimum vacuum extraction requires optimum application and
optimum traction in the direction of the birth canal at the same
time as each uterine contraction.

Traction should be a two-handed exercise. The thumb of the non-pulling hand, pressed firmly against the cup (near its shoulder), keeps the operator in touch with the cup and helps to prevent it from slipping off the scalp. The index finger of the same hand, resting on the shoulder of the cup with the finger tip touching the scalp, monitors descent.

Extraction force should be applied smoothly throughout a contraction and the mother is encouraged to push. Traction is discontinued between contractions. Traction is also discontinued if the cup lifts or if a hiss is heard. The operator must observe the safety rules described below.

Perineotomy

Pre-application perineotomy facilitates good application in occipitoposterior positions. Perineotomy may or may not otherwise be required as in a normal delivery.

The newborn

The vacuum is released and the cup removed once the head is completely delivered. Delivery of the body is completed in the usual way.

Complications

The fetus

The risk of scalp injury is directly related to the number of pulls used, the number of times the cup lifts or becomes completely detached and the duration of the cup's attachment to the scalp. Sudden cup detachments are often abrasive. Jerky, rocking, rotational and oblique pulls, especially when exerted on a badly positioned cup, are not as safe as those that are applied steadily, smoothly and perpendicularly to a cup in the ideal position. Traction that is not strong enough to detach the cup or make the head descend, i.e. **negative traction**, is dangerous because it makes the scalp descend; the galea is pulled away from the skull, and the emissary veins may tear and bleed into the loose subgaleal tissue.

The incidence of intracranial haemorrhage in infants born using VE depends largely on how the instrument is used. Cerebral trauma occurs in about 1.0 per cent of infants when extraction is completed using from one to five pulls; and in about 5.0 per cent when the number of pulls exceeds five.

Perinatal retinal haemorrhages occur in about one-third of infants born spontaneously by the vertex, and are one and a half to two times more frequent when instruments are used to terminate a prolonged second stage of labour.

This increase is due more to the prolonged second stage than to the instrumental delivery itself.

The mother

There is wide agreement that VE is safe for the mother. Any complications that may occur in cases where VE has been applied can rarely be attributed to VE itself, provided the indications are observed and the safety rules respected.

How to avoid complications with VE

There are some fundamental practical principles that must be respected when using VE. These can be summarised as follows:

1. The head must be completely or almost completely delivered with no more than three pulls.

2. The head, not just the scalp, must at least begin to move with the first pull and must definitely advance with each subsequent pull.

3. Mid-cavity and high extractions should be avoided.

4. The cup must not be applied more than twice.

5. The head must be completely delivered within 15 minutes of first applying the cup. Application time must never exceed 20 minutes.

6. VE should not be used with very low birth-weight babies unless for a simple 'lift out'. Forceps should be used if Caesarean section is not available.

Vacuum extraction is no substitute for Caesarean section. **When the latter is not available, however, and it is deemed prudent symphysiotomy should be performed according to good symphysiotomy practice and in combination with careful vacuum extraction. This method will save innumerable lives.**

Appendix III: SYMPHYSIOTOMY

Cutting through the symphysis pubis cartilage as a means of widening the birth canal during protracted deliveries was common in Europe at the turn of the century and has been practised even later. Thanks to improvements in surgery, Caesarean section has, however, become much more common in such situations though symphysiotomy is still practised in situations where neither hygiene nor other material resources permit Caesarean section. It is simple to perform and makes a negligible demand on resources. It is **not**, however, an alternative to routine Caesarean section in general but only in cases with a moderately contracted outlet of the pelvic canal.

Symphysiotomy is controversial most frequently among those who lack personal experience of the method. Documentation[1,2] is today overwhelmingly in favour of symphysiotomy, particularly in situations when there is no access to Caesarean section, as is the case in most rural areas of the world. For later pregnancies, after a Caesarean section, the pelvis remains narrow and the woman is left with a uterine scar. Approximately 25 per cent of uterine ruptures can be estimated to be caused by ruptures of old Caesarean section scars. The risk of maternal death in vaginal deliveries after a delivery by Caesarean section (for disproportion) is thus obvious. Culturally, obstructed labour is sometimes branded as a punishment for infidelity and Caesarean section is often regarded as a reproductive failure on the part of the woman. Once operated upon, the woman may not feel willing to return for a new Caesarean section.

Symphysiotomy is less dangerous than Caesarean section in countries where resources are minimal. Mortality figures of around 1-3 per cent are common in conjunction with Caesarean section in developing countries. Symphysiotomy may be useful under such conditions. Its use can be expected to increase since third world women of fertile age suffer from the effects of early malnutrition, short stature and small pelvis due to stunting. An improvement in the general health standard in certain populations of developing countries, with a resulting increase in birthweight, thus increases the risk of feto-maternal disproportion.

The obstetric situation where a mother suffering from obstructed labour consults a small, remote hospital after perhaps three to four days of labour, illustrates the value of symphysiotomy. The mother's condition is as a rule poor due to anaemia and extreme exhaustion. Symphysiotomy may save the life of both mother and child in such a situation.

It is important to underscore that the normal **symphysiolysis** occurring at the end of pregnancy allows the pelvis to achieve a certain elasticity, facilitating the passage of the fetus. This **stretching of the pelvis** is indispensable for birth in the same way as is **stretching of the perineum**. In both tissue areas, however, the need for surgical support may be indicated and **symphysiotomy** may be considered as an analogy to **perineotomy** (episiotomy).

The problem with symphysiotomy is hardly a technical one: the difficulty lies first and foremost in deciding **at what point** during delivery the operation should be carried out. A fundamental precondition for symphysiotomy is that disproportion actually exists and manifests itself clinically.

Indications

As a result of the varying access to resources at any particular maternity unit in a developing country indications and contraindications are very relative. Certain broad outlines can, however, be laid down.

In general terms it can be stated that symphysiotomy is indicated in an obstructed labour due to a limited feto-pelvic disproportion that may be overcome by surgical widening of the symphysis (up to 2.5 cm). The most clear-cut example of proper indication is the situation with fully dilated cervix, the fetal head at or below the spinal level and unsuccessful vacuum extraction in spite of adequate maternal expulsion efforts.

Degree of disproportion

Symphysiotomy is indicated when obstructed labour is due to a **moderate disproportion** between the fetus and the birth canal. It is felt that major constrictions of the pelvis (true conjugate less than 8 cm) render symphysiotomy unsuitable, even if all remaining preconditions for such an operation exist. In the same way, an asymmetrical pelvis is also an unsuitable indication for symphysiotomy. Suspicion that a child has a weight more than 4500 grams also makes this operation less suitable. A general rule is that labour should have progressed so far that at least a third of the head has passed the pelvic inlet.

A clinically valuable observation for the assessment of progress of labour is the degree of **bulge** above the symphysis pubis. Different degrees of bulge can be felt when the palm of the observer's hand is placed just above the anterior surface of the symphysis pubis: with the **first** degree, the presenting part of the fetus cannot be felt; with the **second**, it can hardly be felt in the palm of the hand; with the **third** degree it can be clearly felt. Symphysiotomy should not be carried out with a third degree bulge (implying an advanced degree of disproportion).

Cervical dilation

The cervix should be completely effaced and dilated to **at least 5 cm in diameter for a woman who has previously given birth** and to **7 cm for a nullipara**. Such requirements are at the same time an expression of the fact that the disproportion between the fetus and the birth canal is moderate. It can be expected that the presenting part of the fetus will descend relatively quickly towards the pelvic floor after symphysiotomy and that the cervix will dilate quickly under such conditions.

Fetal position

The presenting part should ideally be the **head**, in vertex presentation. Face presentation may be accepted though subsequent use of a vacuum extractor is thereby prohibited. Symphysiotomy can be carried out in certain **breech cases** but only with an aftercoming head[3]. The speed with which the operation must be conducted in such cases necessitates an experienced operating surgeon.

The urgency also increases the risk of lesion of the bladder and urethra, particularly since the urethra in these cases cannot be moved digitally from the midline. As an alternative and complement to using forceps on the aftercoming head in breech presentation, symphysiotomy has thus been shown to be of value.

The child's condition

The child should be **alive**. In case of **intrauterine fetal death** a destructive operation (craniotomy etc.) should be performed and symphysiotomy avoided.

Contraindications

Previous Caesarean section constitutes a contraindication for symphysiotomy if there is a real choice between Caesarean section and symphysiotomy. **Musculo-skeletal disorders,** particularly hip, back or knee complaints are other contraindications.

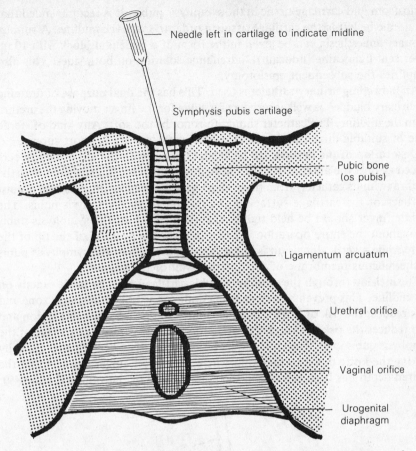

Needle left in cartilage to indicate midline

Symphysis pubis cartilage

Pubic bone
(os pubis)

Ligamentum arcuatum

Urethral orifice

Vaginal orifice

Urogenital
diaphragm

Figure 48 The above diagrammatic illustration shows the main features of the symphysis pubis anatomy. The strength of the cartilage is guaranteed by the area above the ligamentum arcuatum, which comprises the boundary to the urogenital diaphragm. It is extremely important that the urogenital diaphragm is not touched during symphysiotomy due to the risk of damage to the urethral area. The ligamentum arcuatum should therefore not be cut through during symphysiotomy.

Technique

A precondition for the operation is that **the anatomy** of the symphysis pubis area and urogenital diaphragm is fully understood by the individual performing the intervention (see Figure 48).

The patient is placed in the usual gynaecological position with the hip joints slightly abducted, the maximum angle being 90° between the thighs. A substantial **infiltration anaesthesia** should be given in the midline down to the periosteum and cartilage tissue in the symphysis pubis. It is recommended that the needle be left in the cartilage tissue in order to mark the midline. A supplementary anaesthesia can be given in the form of a **pudendal block** with 10 ml 1 per cent lignocaine (lidocain) – adrenaline solution on both sides. This also simplifies the subsequent episiotomy.

An **indwelling urinary catheter** is used. This has **the dual purpose** of draining the urinary bladder as well as serving as a **guide** for the finger moving the urethra from the midline. The catheter should thus not be too soft. Any kind of sterile tube of suitable dimensions can be used if catheters are in short supply.

Dislocation of the urethra can be brought about with the aid of two fingers placed against the anterior wall of the vagina. The index finger then moves the urethra (with its catheter) from the midline while the middle finger is held against the back of the cartilage surface in the midline of the symphysis pubis. The middle finger should be held tightly against the back of the symphysis pubis throughout the entire operation in order to show the position of the tip of the knife while a vertical incision is made through the skin of the symphysis pubis to the mucous membrane of the anterior wall of the vagina.

The **incision** through the symphysis pubis cartilage must be made **exactly** on the midline. This prevents damage being done to the bone – cartilage zone and thus reduces the risk of osteitis and bleeding in the symphysis pubis region and also reduces the risk of bridging ossification (synostosis) in the cartilage of the symphysis pubis joint. The knife should be inserted perpendicularly to the skin by sinking the knife down to the point where the middle finger can feel that the desired depth has been reached in the anterior wall of the vagina (Figure 49).

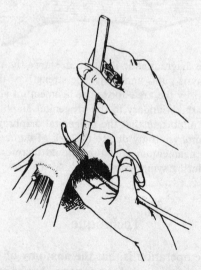

Figure 49   With a catheter in the urethra, it is extremely important that the urethra is dislocated laterally before the incision is made. The urethra is shifted to the patient's left or right side and an incision is prepared on the boundary between the upper and central third of the cartilage tissue in the symphysis pubis.

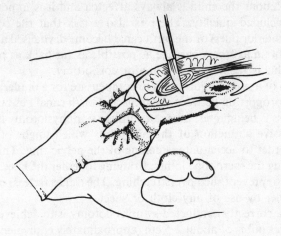

Figure 50   View from the side: the knife can be seen to have penetrated
through the cartilage (perpendicular to the skin). The index finger
feels the penetration through the anterior vaginal mucosa. The
point of the knife should cut right through the cartilage tissue
down close to the mucous membrane of the vagina so that the
finger placed in the vagina and resting against the rear part of the
symphysis pubis can just feel the point of the knife. By drawing
the knife **handle** slowly upwards, most of the **lower** cartilage joint
is cut off. The knife should then be withdrawn, turned 180°, and
re-inserted in the same incision after which the knife handle
should be lowered slowly without cutting off the whole of the
upper third of the symphysis pubis cartilage.

The incision should be made between the upper and central third of the
symphysis pubis cartilage (Figure 50). By rotating the **knife handle upwards**
the two lower thirds of the symphysis pubis cartilage can be cut through, making
sure that the cut finishes at the ligamentum arcuatum (compare Figure 48) and
does not extend as far as the urogenital diaphragm.

Once this part of the operation has been carried out, the knife should be
withdrawn, turned 180° and inserted in the same incision so that the tip of the
knife can once again be felt with the middle finger. By **lowering** the handle,
an equivalent cut will be made in the upper part of the symphysis pubis cartilage,
although **it is advisable at the beginning not to cut right through the whole
cartilage**. Instead, leave approximately 5 mm at the upper end of the joint. This
radically reduces the degree to which the symphysis pubis joint is widened. The
pressure from the fetal presenting part against the pelvic walls usually causes
a slow widening of the symphysis pubis to the desired width. This carries a
smaller risk of laceration to the anterior wall of the birth canal than when the
joint widens quickly.

Vacuum extraction is advisable as a means of concluding the delivery. **Forceps
should not be used** due to the risk of further damage to the soft tissues.

Episiotomy should always be performed in connection with symphysiotomy.

In obstructed labour the child is always affected and it is important that the delivery is concluded quickly. There is also a risk that the soft tissues (in particular the anterior ones) of the birth canal become devitalised and it is always advisable to obtain as free a passage as possible as far **back** as possible in the birth canal. This is facilitated by a major episiotomy.

The purpose of a symphysiotomy is to compensate for a **moderate** disproportion. If the disproportion between the fetus and birth canal has been misjudged and no progress is being made after a complete symphysiotomy it is **important to avoid excessive abduction of the hip joints** which might otherwise seem motivated in order to accentuate widening of the pelvic ring. This has the risk of overstretching the sacro-iliac joints. Bringing together the knees is sometimes recommended to prevent such overstretching. The thighs (knees) may be loosely brought together by use of any cloth or sheet.

The aim of a correctly conducted symphysiotomy is to achieve a separation of the symphysis pubis of about 2.5 cm (approximately equivalent to the width of thumb), thereby increasing the surface area of the pelvic inlet by approximately 20-25 per cent. If no progress occurs despite this increase a more advanced disproportion is probable. Successful vaginal delivery is unlikely and Caesarean section will be the only alternative.

It should be kept in mind that symphysiotomy which unexpectedly results in failure may well be followed by Caesarean section, provided the fetus is alive. If no fetal heart sounds can be heard, craniotomy is recommended.

Aftercare

An indwelling catheter should be left in the bladder after the operation only if there is haematuria. The use of catheters should be limited due to the danger of urinary tract infection. Haematuria may be a sign of early fistulation and a general rule is to leave the catheter in for a few days once the haematuria has cleared up.

Confinement to bed is recommended for approximately 3 days, preferably with the patient lying on her side. She may then sit or lie for 2 days, getting on her feet on the fifth day post-partum. A total of 7 days' hospital care is usually sufficient.

In cases of instability and motion pains a **bandage** (trochanter bandage) may be advisable while the patient is confined to bed, and possibly for an even longer period.

Complications

Experience shows that symphysiotomy is associated with almost negligible mortality.

Post-operative **stress incontinence** may occur in a few percent of operated cases. Check-ups of women who have undergone symphysiotomy show that stress incontinence is permanent in about 3 per cent of cases. The equivalent figure for Caesarean section cases under similar conditions is about 2 per cent.

Fistulae at the urethrovaginal or vesicovaginal level rarely occur when symphysiotomy has been correctly carried out. As already mentioned, episiotomy is a good prophylaxis. If a fistula is caused by the symphysiotomy itself the chances of its healing are good using only an indwelling catheter since the tissues are not devitalised in the same way as when the fistulation is caused by fetal pressure on the birth canal. According to results published fistulation occurs in approximately 0.5 per cent of cases.

Post-operative **difficulty in walking** may be caused by some pain and discomfort. According to reports published, difficulty in walking is rare more than 2 months after symphysiotomy.

Back pain post-partum seems to be more common after Caesarean section than after symphysiotomy. Back pains are probably connected to overstretching of the sacro-iliac joints. This can be prevented by employing a strict upper abduction limit of the hip joints during the operation and by adducting the knees between symphysiotomy and the delivery proper.

Prognosis

In most cases, a symphysiotomy is considered to enlarge the pelvic inlet permanently and subsequent deliveries are usually easier. The cut in the cartilage joint normally heals with a fibrous tissue, which is considered to be stronger than the original cartilage tissue. A symphysiotomy can, however, be carried out even if the urethra lies adherent to the rear of the area being operated on. The urethra will, however, be particularly vulnerable in a subsequent symphysiotomy. In certain cases an ossification of parts of the symphysis pubis joint can also be seen. This can render a renewed symphysiotomy more difficult. Remaining, late morbidity of any significance occurs in approximately 2 per cent of patients who have undergone symphysiotomy.

REFERENCES

1. Gebbie, D.A.M. Symphysiotomy. In: Philpott, R.H. (ed.) *Clinical Obstetrics and Gynecology* 1982; **9**: 663-83.

2. van Roosmalen, J. Safe motherhood: Caesarean section or symphysiotomy. *American Journal of Obstetrics and Gynecology* 1990; **163**: 1-4.

3. Spencer, J.A.D. Symphysiotomy for vaginal breech delivery. Two case reports. *British Journal of Obstetrics and Gynaecology* 1987; **94**: 716-18.

Appendix IV: CAESAREAN SECTION UNDER LOCAL ANAESTHESIA

It is difficult to establish an optimum rate of Caesarean section (CS) in a given society. Internationally the trend is that CS is on the increase. There are both medical and commercial reasons for this. If the objective is to minimise perinatal infant and maternal mortality/morbidity, the CS rate can be kept low, very often around 5 per cent while achieving an acceptably low level of mortality/morbidity. In commercialised obstetrics in more affluent societies one of the major problems is alleged malpractice/mismanagement. Both fear of legal consequences after a complicated vaginal delivery and economic incentives of choosing abdominal delivery as opposed to vaginal tend to increase the CS rate.

International comparisons have clearly shown that there has been no parallel improvement in perinatal mortality with the steep increase in CS rate (see Figure 51). In some Latin American countries and in the US the very high CS rate tends to set the pattern for the elite of many developing countries. This is most undesirable, since it implies wastage of human and material resources, increased risks for the mothers and non-scientific obstetrical practice. An increasing number of unnecessary CSs will also lead to an increasing number of unnecessarily ruptured uteruses in subsequent pregnancies.

In many cultures CS is regarded as a reproductive defeat. There is a high risk that such women will not come back for institutional (abdominal) delivery and will give birth at home, with an increased risk of uterine rupture.

Indications

The general indications for emergency CS are listed here. They are not specifically alluded to in the context of local anaesthesia (described below) but rather as a background.

Mechanical dystocia constitutes one of the most frequent indications of CS. The concept has been defined in Chapter 7.

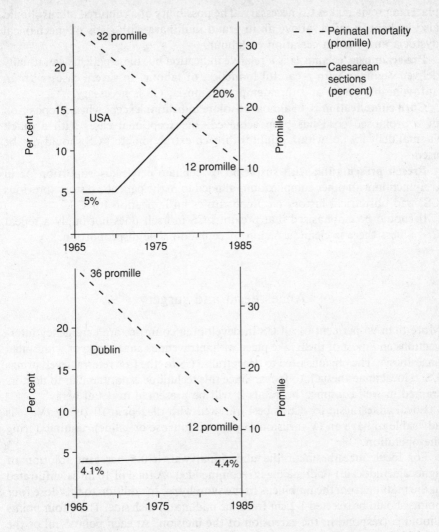

Figure 51 The upper diagram reflects the tendency in the USA towards high
frequency of Caesarean sections, while the lower diagram shows
the situation in Dublin, Ireland where a very low frequency of
Caesarean sections has been maintained. The perinatal mortality
has undergone a more or less identical development in Ireland
and in the USA.

Severe intrauterine asphyxia before the expulsion phase motivates urgent
delivery by CS. The diagnosis is suspected when there is repeated late slowings
of the heartbeat (fetal bradycardia) which does not return to normal in either
the left or right supine positions or with access to oxygen.

Vaginal bleeding indicates use of CS, provided the total clinical situation
makes vaginal delivery impossible. Suspicion of severe abruptio placentae or

placenta previa makes CS necessary. The possibility of a ruptured uterus should also be kept in mind, above all in grand multipara with signs of mechanical dystocia and sudden cessation of labour.

Pre-eclampsia/eclampsia is a relative indication but these patients can usually deliver vaginally with a careful induction of labour. In severe cases with an unfavourable cervix and threatening eclampsia, CS is necessary.

Cord complication is an almost absolute indication except when a reposition of a prolapsed cord has been achieved. In exceptional cases with a quick vaginal delivery i.e. within minutes (breech extraction etc.) CS should not be used.

Breech presentation with suspicion of cephalo-pelvic disproportion or in conjunction with other complications alluded to in the patient's history (previous CS, bad obstetrical history etc.) constitutes an indication for CS.

It should be emphasised that previous CS in itself does not imply a repeat CS, unless there is clear suspicion of cephalo-pelvic disproportion.

Anaesthesia and surgery

More than 95 per cent of all CS in developing countries are emergency interventions and most of them take place with intravenous anaesthesia or with spinal anaesthesia. The obvious need to decentralise CS to 'the first referral level' brings CS in local anaesthesia into focus. Since this technique is not familiar to doctors trained in well-equipped hospitals it will be presented in detail here.

Local anaesthesia for CS is best initiated with diazepam 10-20 mg IV. It is advisable to have an IV infusion (5 per cent glucose or saline) running during the operation.

For local anaesthesia of the abdominal wall a 0.5 per cent solution of lignocaine(lidocain) – adrenaline is recommended. A total of 10 ml is infiltrated in the midline from the umbilicus to the symphysis. In addition to this dose four points should be selected 1-2 cm from the midline on each side. These four points should correspond to the extension of the incision. At each point 5 ml of the solution is injected to reach the rectus sheath, and the total amount therein should then amount to 8×5 or 40 ml. Once this infiltration is complete, the abdominal wall is cut open down to the linea alba. Some 20 ml of the solution are infiltrated through the midline and in the parietal peritoneum immediately below the linea alba along the planned incision. The peritoneal cavity is opened and about 5-10 ml infiltrated just above the upper border of the bladder along the line of peritoneal incision. If pain is provoked on the upper part of the symphysis a few millilitres of solution are then injected into the rectus insertion in the superior pubic periosteum.

Hysterotomy is carried out after the bladder peritoneum has been separated and forced somewhat downwards. At this stage about 80 ml (400 mg lignocaine chloride (lidocain)) have been given. This is below the recommended maximum dose of 500 mg. The obvious disadvantage of local anaesthesia is that the visceral peritoneum of all other organs close to the uterus is painful. Utmost care should therefore be taken in order not to cause unnecessary pain.

A good alternative to infiltration anaesthesia is spinal anaesthesia. In some cases, however, the patient's circulation may be in danger and any hypotension provoked by a spinal anaesthesia may be unacceptable. This is particularly true in desolate cases of premature detachment of the placenta, heavy bleeding or other situations giving rise to hypovolemic shock.

Infection prophylaxis

In most situations it is advisable to give antibiotic protection per-operatively (during the operation). A distinction should be made between 'clean' and 'dirty' CS. The former include cases operated upon electively or with clinically intact membranes without any clinical suspicion of pre-existing infections (long-standing rupture of membranes, foul-smelling vaginal discharge etc.). In such cases the need for antibiotics is small but in most places the routine is to give benzylpenicillin (penicillin G) 3.3 g (5,000,000 IU) intravenously at the beginning of the operation. Two doses of the same drug amounting to 1.3 g (2,000,000 IU) are then given intravenously 6 and 12 hours post-operatively.

'Dirty' (infected) cases comprise those with ruptured membranes for more than 4 hours or cases with clinical signs of intrauterine infection, fever, foul-smelling amniotic fluid or uterine tenderness.

The per-operative dose comprises benzylpenicillin 3.3 g (5,000,000 IU (alternatively chloramphenicol 1 g IV). After the operation benzylpenicillin, 1.3 g (2,000,000 IU) is given intravenously every 8 hours (alternatively chloramphenicol 0.5 g IV) for 7 days. Another alternative is to give metronidazole in tablet form dissolved in a suitable liquid and given rectally in a dose of 800 mg every 8 hours, (corresponding to 2.5 g per 24 hours per rectum). The latter method will give metronidazole concentrations very close to serum levels after IV infusion of the same drug. Economically and practically this administration has clear advantages.

Post-operative morbidity

The predominant postoperative complications are intrauterine infection (endometritis – myometritis) or wound infection. Such infections can usually be treated successfully with the above antibiotic prophylaxis complemented by a suitable broad spectrum of antibiotics, chloramphenicol or metronidazole.

There is no reason to utilise methylergometrine or other drugs bringing about uterine contractions in cases of endometritis – myometritis, neither after CS nor after vaginal delivery. These drugs presumably decrease the perfusion of the infected uterus and will probably diminish the effect of antibiotic drugs.

Abdominal wall infections often lead to suture insufficiency and such wounds should be cut open as soon as infection is suspected. The wound should be left open down to the fascia, with a sterile saline dressing in the wound. On the sixth or seventh post-operative day the wound is inspected and, if clean, the edges adapted and sutured. The patient can be discharged from the hospital the same day and should return 1 week later for a check-up.

Appendix V: BLOOD EXCHANGE TRANSFUSION

Purpose

The **purpose** of the treatment is: to reduce both anaemia and the number of red cells that would otherwise be haemolised by the mother's antibodies, and to combat hyperbilirubinaemia.

The indication is thus a new-born baby (with a positive Coombs' test if possible) with severe anaemia, a haemoglobin level below 12 g per cent and rapidly developing jaundice over the first 24 hours after birth. The blood volume used is twice the blood volume of the baby, or 150-200 ml/kg body weight. Fresh O Rh negative citrated blood is used.

Technique

Cut the umbilical cord about 0.5 cm from the skin. Clean it properly and cover the skin with a sterile cloth. The vein is easily seen in the upper part of the umbilicus. It is much wider than the two arteries. Introduce a plastic catheter gently about 7-8 cm until free flow of blood is obtained.

Remove about 15-20 ml of blood into a 20 ml syringe. Close the catheter, discard the blood and replace it with donor's blood. This procedure is repeated until the blood volume calculated has been exchanged. Keep a careful record of the volume of the blood being used and the duration of the procedure. An assistant must be assigned to note each time the syringe is emptied.

Monitor the heart rate continuously with a stethoscope or electrocardiogram. If vomiting or bradycardia occur stop the procedure. It is the infusion rate that is critical: infusion must be slow with 5-10 ml being infused over a minute. The most dangerous complication is a severe bradycardia and apnoea. Should this occur, it can almost always be handled by proper resuscitation using bag and mask ventilation and external cardiac compressions.

After removing the catheter it is often not necessary to suture the umbilical vein: a sterile cloth placed on the vein for some hours is sufficient.

Septicaemia may occur in conditions where sterility is poor. Under these conditions prophylactic treatment with penicillin after exchange transfusion might be indicated.

Appendix VI: POST-PARTUM FAMILY PLANNING

Family planning is a component of perinatal health care. It is essential that a mother has a period of rest and recovery after a birth. There are several reasons for offering a contraceptive to mothers before they leave a health institution after a delivery:

1. It will guarantee the mother a period of recovery during breast feeding.

2. It will avoid the competition between the breast-fed baby and the fetus of a new pregnancy.

3. It will help to guarantee that the health of the family is not threatened by too many births too close together.

4. It will give the woman a possibility of choosing whether or not to get pregnant.

In most cultures there is a protective period of sexual abstinence after delivery. The cervix is particularly vulnerable the first weeks after delivery and post-partum infection (endometritis – myometritis) may occur as a result of ascending infections related to sexual intercourse. If there is no cultural taboo against sexual intercourse after delivery, it is advisable to postpone any sexual intercourse till at least 6 weeks after delivery. It has been said that breast-feeding is the world's most important contraceptive. It is true that there is no method that prevents as many births as breast-feeding at a global level. At the individual mother's level breast-feeding will be an important basis protecting against a new pregnancy.

Frequent breast-feeding on demand by the baby will make ovulation improbable during the first 6-8 months. If there is no breast-feeding at all the first post-partum ovulation may take place 5-6 weeks after birth. Even if breast-feeding is an important contraceptive it should be emphasised that it is not sufficient for the protection of the woman and an additional contraceptive is always advisable after a couple of months' breast-feeding.

For the breast-feeding mother the choice of contraceptive is crucial and it is important to give the best advice to these mothers in order to protect both the mother against a new pregnancy and protect the baby by guaranteeing lactation. The following short review is given regarding advisable contraceptive methods in the post-partum period.

Condoms

If culturally acceptable condoms are one of the best methods, since they protect against pregnancy and also against infection. Much effort should be given to promote this method in maternal health education and in the mass media. Its importance for protection against HIV infection is well known.

Oral contraception

The normal 'pill' should not be utilised after birth, since it counteracts breast-milk production. This refers to the combined pill, containing both oestrogen and gestagen. The only pill that should be used when breast-feeding is the mini-pill. This pill contains only gestagen and will not disturb breast-feeding. This 'one component only' preparation is similar to the contraceptive injection (Depo-Provera).

The mini-pill can be given directly after birth but it is advisable to start later. Provided there is efficient and frequent breast-feeding it may be better to start at 4-6 months post partum.

Injectables

This group of drugs is dominated by Depo-Provera® , which is given in a dose of 150 mg every 3 months. In most women it will give bleeding disturbances but it is otherwise well accepted in most cultures. Information about these menstrual disturbances should be given to each woman receiving injections. As far as is known so far these injectables do not influence breast-feeding adversely. New injectables with oestrogen tend, however, to appear on the market and such injectables should not be given during breast-feeding. It is therefore important to see that injectables contain only the gestagen component.

Intrauterine device (IUD)

If IUDs are acceptable in the local population and if the risk of infection in the individual woman is considered low, an IUD may be a safe alternative. It is advisable to postpone insertion till 8-12 weeks post-partum and the insertion should be made with utmost care, since, with well-functioning breast-feeding the oestrogen levels in the woman may be low and the uterus quite small. It is therefore most important to palpate of the uterus before insertion to assess the uterine size and position (corpus bent forward – anteflexion, or backward – retroflexion).

Tubal ligation

In many instances tubal ligation post-partum is an ideal contraceptive choice, particularly in grand multiparous women. In the simplest version this intervention can be made under local anaesthesia. A puerperal woman who has expressed the desire to have tubal ligation can easily be helped by carrying out this intervention before discharge from a health unit after birth.

Tubal sterilisation is easily performed with local anaesthesia within the first 2 weeks after delivery. The uterus is easily accessible in the abdominal cavity, thus facilitating the operation. If more than 2 weeks have passed after delivery the use of a uterine elevator is recommended. One appropriate technique, if no uterine elevator is available, is to pack the vagina with gauze. It will thereby become 'erect' and make the uterus better positioned for the operation.

The patient and her husband should be well-informed, before the operation, about the irreversible character of the sterilisation. Even if careful microsurgical techniques can be quite successful, such reversibility is seldom available in practice.

The woman should fast overnight in preparation for general anaesthesia, should this be necessary. Premedication is useful and diazepam 10 mg IV and pethidine 50mg IM are recommended 30 min before the operation. It is imperative that the patient has an empty bladder immediately before the operation.

An intravenous line should be established and a saline drip, where available, should be given to maintain the needle. The patient should preferably lie in the supine position. If the uterine elevator is used the woman should be in a gynaecological examination position.

Depending on the palpated level of the uterine fundus a transverse (or midline) skin incision in planned. A 0.5 per cent lignocaine(lidocain) – adrenaline solution is preferable. The total volume given of this anaesthetic in tubal ligation should not exceed 60 ml (corresponding to 300 mg of lignocaine chloride (lidocain)). The skin is infiltrated covering a planned incision length of 5 cm at the fundus level. This first infiltrate should reach the fascia. After a couple of minutes the skin is opened and the fascia is infiltrated including the subfascial peritoneum.

The fascia and the peritoneum are then opened.

The anatomy of the junction of the tube and the uterus must be well understood. There are three structures entering the uterus at this junction. The tube is in the middle. Behind it is the ligament going to the ovary. In front of it is the round ligament going towards the inguinal canal. After identification of the tubes, they should be infiltrated bilaterally at their most accessible points. The anaesthetized part of the tube is then grasped and brought into the operation field by gentle traction. Careful identification of the tube at its junction with the uterus is mandatory. If judged necessary more anaesthesia is infiltrated around the site of ligation. A tubal sling is then excised using the Pomeroy technique. The same procedure is carried out on the opposite side. It is imperative that the ligature (preferably silk but catgut is an alternative) is firmly placed and sutured to the peritubal tissue. Bleeding should be controlled and each abdominal wall layer should then be closed by catgut.

A number of clinical conditions may make the use of local anaesthesia less desirable. Previous laparotomy may make a small incision difficult and a larger incision (requiring general anaesthesia) may be necessary. In general, previous laparotomy constitutes a relative contraindication to the use of local anaesthesia. Obesity also constitutes a relative contraindication, since thick adipose layers are difficult to infiltrate with a local anaesthetic solution. Exposure of the tubouterine junction may also be difficult due to thick adipose layers. Allergy to local anaesthetic is an absolute contraindication to the use of such drugs. Post-delivery complications such as bleeding, fever etc. are relative contraindications.

Post-operative care

It is advisable for the patient to rest for 2 days at home. If the operation is carried out immediately post-partum she should avoid strenuous lifting for 1 week. The rate of complications is low, below 1 per cent, comprising infections, haematoma, uterine lacerations (if elevators are used), occasional bladder injury and sterilisation failure.

Index

abdomen
  aortic compression 65, 67, 90-1
  bleeding 40
  infections 176
abdominal pregnancy 57
abortion, infection 120
abruptio placentae 66-7
acyclovir (AZT) 131
adrenaline 86
AIDS 129-31, 137
airways, cleaning 32, 33, 80, 82
aminoglycoside 140
amniotic fluid infection syndrome (AFIS) 122-3
ampicillin 140
anaemia 13, 14, 42, 46-8, 90, 126
anaesthesia, for Caesarean section 174-5
antenatal card 19-21, 148
antenatal care 10-19, 146
  early booking 10
  preventive 142
  risk approach 10-18
  urban/rural differences 12
antibiotics 97, 139-40
antimalarials 126
anuria 94
aortic compression 65, 67, 90-1
apnoeic spells 116
areflexia 71
arm-movement, asymmetrical 116
arthritis 133
asphyxia 78-87, 117, 151-2, 160, 173
auscultation 30, 70

baby: see neonate; newborn
back pain 171
bacterial infection, newborn 39, 133-4
bag and mask resuscitation 85, 87

Bandl's furrow 60
Bangladesh, maternal mortality 4, 6
BCG vaccination 38
benzylpenicillin 72, 128, 140, 175
bilharzia 15, 92
birth asphyxia 78-87
birth assistant 25; see also traditional birth attendant
birth complications 59-77
birth trauma 118-19
birth weight 4, 36, 51-2, 97-101, 156
birthing position 25-6, 144
bladder 93, 135-6
bleeding
  abdominal 40
  anaemia 90-1
  lacerations 68-9
  uterus 67-9
  vaginal 40, 41, 173-4
blood bank 148
blood exchange transfusion 91, 115, 177-8
blood group incompatibility 113
blood pressure 13, 15, 41, 42, 70; see also hypertension
bottle feeding 110
bradycardia 86
Brazil, poverty 5
breast milk
  colostrum 39, 43, 107-8
  consumption 111
  donated 110
  expressed 109
  human 108, 109
  inadequate 109
  jaundice 114
breast-feeding 42-4
  and AIDS 130
  contraceptive effect 3, 179
  diarrhoea avoidance 137
  drugs 109
  early 33
  nipples 44, 109

  and oral contraception 180
  as prophylactic measure 138
  sick babies 107-9
breech presentation 17, 54, 55, 62-3, 174
buffalo milk 110
buffer solution, intravenous 86

Caesarean section 61, 67, 164, 172-6
cardiac massage, external 86
cerebral infections 117
cerebral malaria 71-2, 126
cerebrovascular complications 72-3
cervical cancer 57
cervicogram 28-30, 148
cervix 25, 28, 74, 166
chlamydia 92
chloramphenicol 72, 175
chlorhexidine 34
chloroquine 72, 126
chlorpromazine 76, 125
cholestatic jaundice 114
circulatory disorders 36
cleft palate 37
coagulopathy 67
colostrum 39, 43, 107-8
community support 146
condoms 180
congenital pneumonia 96
congenital syphilis 128
conjunctivitis 129, 133
continuous positive airway pressure (CPAP) 96-7
contraceptives 179-80
contractions 28
convulsions 70-3, 116-18
Coombs' test 113
cord: see umbilical cord
cough 16
cows' milk 110
craniotomy 166, 170
crying, abnormal 116
cultural traditions and beliefs 23, 164

183

cyanosis 95

delivery care 26-8, 147-51; *see also* home deliveries
delivery record sheet 150
delivery ward book 148-9
demand feeding 44
Depo-Provera 180
diazepam 69, 71, 117, 174, 181
dihydrolizine 51, 69
dilatation 25, 28
disinfectant 131
disproportion 165-6
doctors 146
doula 23-4
drop foot 60
drugs, while breast-feeding 109
dystocia 28, 59-62, 172

eclampsia 4, 50-1, 70-1, 93, 174
ectopic pregnancy 57
education, girls and women 3, 6, 7
endometritis-myometritis 91-2, 124, 179
endotracheal tube 85
engorgement 109
epiphysiolysis 118, 136
episiotomy 162, 165, 169

family planning 179-82
fathers 8, 44-5
feeding techniques, newborn 39, 110
fetus
    death 58, 61
    growth 17
    heart auscultation 30, 70
    infection, routes 122
    monitoring 30
    movement 53
    position, symphysiotomy 166
    presentations 17, 62-4
fever, puerperal infection 41-2
fibrinolysis 67
Finnström maturation score 102
fistula 60, 93, 170, 171
fits 70-3, 116-18
floppiness 116
folic acid 18, 19, 47
fractures 118
fundal pressure 68-9

Gambia, nutrition supplements 49
gastroenteritis 137

gavage feeding 111, 125
gentamycin 140
gestational age 101, 156
glucose 111
glucose-6-phosphate-dehydrogenase 114
gonorrhoea 38, 92, 129
growth retardation 53, 98-100, 126
Guatemala, birth attendants 23-4

haematuria 93, 170
haemoglobin defects 47
haemorrhage
    intercranial 117, 162
    maternal 4, 56-7
    perinatal retinal 162
    subaponeurotic 118
hand washing 138
head size 115
health education 8-10, 44-5
hearing, impaired 116
heart beat, newborn 80
heat loss, newborn 32
hepatitis B 132
hexachlorophane 34
HIV 19, 91, 110, 129-31, 137
home deliveries 23-4, 26, 27, 142-5
hookworm 18-19, 47
hyaline membrane disease 95-6
hydralazine 51, 69
hydrocephalus 116
hygiene
    during delivery 121-2, 137-8
    home deliveries 26-7, 142
    infections 41
    newborn 138
    umbilical cord 133
hyperbilirubinaemia 113, 177
hyperoxia 97
hyperreflexia 69, 71
hypertension 42, 50-1, 69-70, 93-4
hypocalcaemia 117
hypoglycaemia 117
hypothermia 38-9, 101-7
hypothyroidism, congenital 114
hypovolaemia 90
hypoxia 97, 104
hysterotomy 174

icterometer 113
immunisation 121, 124-5, 137
incontinence 171
incubators 88, 107, 139
induction 123
infant mortality: *see* mortality

infections
    abdomen 176
    abortions 120
    AFIS 122-3
    ascending 120, 121, 123
    bacterial 39, 133-4
    cerebral 117
    newborn 37, 121, 132-7
    perinatal 120, 122-39
    post-delivery 91-2
    prevention 137-8
    prophylaxis 175
    puerperal 41-2, 124
    skin 132-3
    transplacental 121
    umbilical cord 132-3
    vagina 121
injectable contraceptives 180
institutional deliveries 27-8
intermittent positive pressure ventilation (IPPV) 96-7
intracranial haemorrhage 117, 162
intrauterine asphyxia 173
intrauterine device (IUD) 181
intrauterine fetal death 58, 61, 166
intrauterine growth 4, 53, 97-8
intravenous nutrition 111
intubation 85
iron 18, 47, 111
irritability, newborn 116
ischaemia 60

jaundice 112-15
jitters, newborn 116

kangaroo method 33, 105, 106
keratitis 129
kernicterus 114-15, 117

labour 28-31, 51-3
lacerations, bleeding 68-9
laparotomy 67, 69, 182
live birth 157
lobeline 86
low birth weight 4, 36, 51-2, 97-101, 156
lumbar puncture 72, 73, 135

magnesium sulphate 51, 70, 71, 94
malaria 19, 47, 125-7
malformations 37, 115
malnutrition 3, 4, 5, 16, 48-9
manual extraction 64
mastitis 44, 91
maternal bonding 32-3, 38
maternal mortality 4, 6, 158

maternal perinatal infections 122-4
mattress, water-filled 106
maturation scoring system 101, 102
meconium aspiration 96, 99-100
medical assistants 145-6
medical history, antibiotics 139-40
membrane rupture 53, 64, 123, 137
meningitis 72, 117, 133, 134-5
mental disease, puerperium 76
metabolism, and cooling 103-4
metronidazole 175
microcephalus 115-16
mid-upper-arm circumference 16
midwives 145, 154
milk: *see* breast milk
milk formula 110, 111
morbidity, post-operative 175-6
mortality
  fetal 58, 61, 166
  maternal 4, 6, 158
  neonatal 1, 2-3, 157-8
  perinatal 150, 156, 157, 158, 172
mother 10-18, 120, 147
mother-baby bonding 32-3, 38, 105
mouth to mouth ventilation 84
multiparity 13, 62
multiple pregnancy 18

naloxone 86
nasal catheter 96
necrosis, subcutaneous fat 118
neonatal asphyxia 99-100
neonatal care 39, 101-7, 151-2
neonatal deaths 1, 2-3, 157-8
neonatal hypoglycaemia 99
neonatal tetanus 116, 133
neurological disorders 36-7, 115-18
newborn
  bacterial infection 39, 133-4
  breathing 80
  care 32-5
  heart beat 80
  heat loss 32
  infection 37, 121, 132-7
  invasive methods 138
  man-made complications 38-9
  nutrition 39, 107-12
  prophylactic procedures 37-8

second assessment 35-7
transporting 87-8
warming 106
nipples 44, 109
nulliparae, dystocia 62
nurses 145, 154
nutrition 48, 97, 107-12, 137

obstetric deaths, direct/indirect 158
obstetric forceps 159
obstetric malpractice 30-1
obstructed labour 4
oedema 13
ophthalmia neonatorum 129
opisthotonic posture 116
oral contraception 180
oropharyngeal suction 82
osteitis 133
osteochondritis 128
osteomyelitis 136
oxidase test 129
oxygen, supplementary 85
oxytocin 33, 42, 62, 68

parenteral nutrition 111-12
partogram 28, 148
patient's record 142, 148
pelvic floor phase, delay 160
penicillin 92, 125, 129, 140
perinatal care 3, 142-6, 150
perinatal death 150, 156, 157, 158, 172
perinatal health 5-6
perinatal infections
  immune systems 120
  maternal 122-4
  prevention 137-9
  specific maternal and fetal/neonatal 124-37
perinatal period 1-2, 156
perinatal retinal haemorrhage 162
perineotomy 162, 165
pethidine 66, 181
phenobarbital 125
phenobarbitone 87, 117
phenytoin 117-18
phototherapy 114
placenta, retained 75-6
placenta previa 56, 65-6
placental abruption 56-7
pneumonia 91, 96, 136-7
podalic version 64
polio 5
polyps 57
post-asphytic treatment 87
post-delivery infections 91-2
post-operative morbidity 175-6
post-term period 157
potassium 112

poverty 3, 4-5, 13
pre-delivery care, high risk 147
pre-eclampsia 50-1, 69, 90, 93-4, 174
pre-term babies 100-1, 113
pre-term labour 51-3
pre-term period 156-7
pregnancy
  anaemia 46-8
  breech presentation 17, 54, 55, 62-3, 174
  cervical diseases 57
  hypertension 50-1
  illness during 117
  infection prevention 137-8
  intrauterine fetal death 58, 61, 166
  intrauterine growth retardation 4, 53, 97-8
  malnutrition 48-9
  maternal haemorrhage 56-7
  pre-term labour 51-3
  prelabour rupture of membranes 53
  psychological and social aspects 7-8
  registration 2-3
  sexual intercourse 52, 120-1, 179
  twins 54-5, 64, 160
preventive care chain 153
prolactin 42
prolapse conditions 73-5
prophylaxis, and treatment 18-19
proteinuria 15, 69
pseudoparalysis 128
pudendal block 168
puerperal malaria 41
puerperal septicaemia 121
puerperium 40-4
  assessment 40-2
  care 152
  hygiene 26-7
  infections 124
  mental disease 76
  psychosis 76
pulmonary adaption syndrome 95
pyelitis 92
pyelonephritis 133, 135-6
pyrexia 128
pyrimetamine 72

quinine 72, 126

radiant heat, for newborn 106-7
Rapid Plasma Reagin (RPR) 128
registration 2-3, 150-1

reproduction, life card 6
respiratory disorders (RDS)
    36, 95-7
resuscitation 83, 85-6, 87, 152
retroplacental haematoma 66
rickets 5
risk approach, antenatal care
    10-18
rooming-in system 138

salbutamol 74
sepsis 120, 133
septicaemia 4, 41, 117, 133,
    178
sexual behaviour 137
sexual intercourse, pregnancy
    52, 120-1, 179
silver nitrate 38, 129, 133
skin infections, newborn 132-3
skin-to-skin contact 87-8, 105
social risk 18
sodium 111
sodium hypochlorite 131
spoon and cup feeding 110
sterilisation of instruments
    139
steroid treatment 99
stillbirths 1, 2-3, 157
streptomycin 127
stress incontinence 171
stunting 5
subaponeurotic haemorrhage
    118

subtle seizures 116
sucking
    inability 116, 125
    positions 43
    pre-term baby 101
    resuscitation 87
sulphadoxine 72
sulphadoxine-pyrimethamine
    (Fansidar) 126
surfactant, insufficiency 95-6
symphysiotomy 63, 160, 163,
    164-71
symphysis pubis 167
symphysis-fundus measure-
    ment 17, 18, 53
symptomatic bacteraemia 111
syphilis 19, 128-9

tachypnoea 95
terbutaline 74
term period 157
tetanus 19, 124-5
tissue pallor 13, 40
tocolysis 52, 64
toxaemia 50-1
traditional birth attendants
    23, 25, 78, 87, 143-5
traditional practices 7, 34
transplacental infection 121
transport incubator 88
transverse lie 63-4
Trendelenburg position 65
trismus 125

trochanter bandage 170
tubal ligation 181-2
tuberculosis 38, 127
twin births 54-5, 64, 160

umbilical cord
    care 34-5
    infections 132-3
    prolapse 64, 73-4, 174
    transfusion 177
unconsciousness 70-3
UNICEF 2, 43, 124, 155
urethra, dislocation 168
urinary tract diseases 92-3
uterus 41, 60, 68-9, 74-5

vacuum extraction 61, 159-63
vagina 40, 41, 69, 121, 173-4
ventilation, assisted 83-4
venturi valve 96
vitamins 37, 111

warming, newborn 106; *see
    also* hypothermia
wet lung disease 95
wet nurses 109-10
WHO (World Health
    Organization) 2, 10, 43,
    126, 155, 156
women
    education 3, 6, 7, 8-10,
    44-5
    status 2, 7, 153